Analytical Reading Inventory

Fourth Edition

Analytical Reading Inventory

Fourth Edition

Assessing Reading Strategies for:
- Literature/Story
- Science
- Social Studies

For All Students Including Gifted and Remedial

Mary Lynn Woods

Reading Specialist
Orchard Country Day School
Indianapolis, Indiana

Alden J. Moe

Lehigh University

Merrill Publishing Company
A Bell & Howell Information Company
Columbus   Toronto   London   Melbourne

Published by Merrill Publishing Company
A Bell & Howell Information Company
Columbus, Ohio 43216

This book was set in News Gothic.

Administrative Editor: Jeff Johnston
Production Coordinator: Carol Driver
Cover Designer: Brian Deep

Library of Congress Catalog Card Number: 88-62679
International Standard Book Number: 0-675-20655-3
Printed in the United States of America
1 2 3 4 5 6 7 8 9—93 92 91 90 89

DEDICATION

In memory of A. EDSON SMITH,
a dedicated educator and father
of the first author of this text.

Also in memory of SISTER MARY EDWARD DOLAN, PBVM,
who helped the second author construct
his first informal reading inventory.

And to all professionals who
are committed to helping children read.

ACKNOWLEDGMENTS

Sometimes words don't adequately convey the depth of our gratitude to the many individuals involved in the development of this inventory, yet without making acknowledgments the message would go unrecorded. First and foremost, to Katherine, John, and Ken Woods, family of the first author, a most heartfelt thank you for their support through the thick and thin of ten years of writing, revising, and more writing and revising.

A sincere thank you goes to Dr. Helen Felsenthal who encouraged the first author to undertake this project in 1975. To Michael Igo and Anna Sanford for their field testing the inventory with undergraduates, for their use of the inventory in a clinical setting, and for their constructive suggestions for changes, we are most appreciative. To Gloria Brown and Cynthia Pulver for the time and energy expended in analyzing the passages, we are thankful. And to Joan Gipe for field testing the inventory with undergraduates, for her assistance in determining the readability levels of the narrative passages, and for her ability to see that the second author completed his assignments on time, we offer a special thanks.

We wish to express our sincere appreciation to Katherine E. Richmond, University of Florida, Susan Homan, University of South Florida, Ellen Garfinkel, University of Virginia, Bonnie Chambers, Bowling Green State University, Sharon Wooden, New Mexico State University, and Doris E. Jakubeck, Central Washington University, who provided valuable feedback prior to the preparation of the third edition. And in this fourth edition, we extend our gratitude to our current reviewers— Mary Ann Pollock of Morehead State University, Morehead, Kentucky; Barbara Decker of Louisiana State University at Shreveport, Louisiana; Don Hunt of Southeast Missouri State University, Cape Girandeau, Missouri; Madelyn Hanes of the University of South Carolina; and Kate Hathaway of Columbia University Teachers College, New York, New York.

There were many people who helped to provide valuable feedback and support during the preparation of the fourth edition. To Susan Robinson, School 39, Indianapolis, Indiana, and Debbie Fuller, Washington Township Public Schools, Indianapolis, Indiana, who provided invaluable feedback for decisions related to content area material, the first author holds the highest regard for their professional opinions and personal friendships. To the teachers and students of Orchard Country Day School, Indianapolis—specifically, Mrs. Colip's second grade, Mrs. Ayres' third grade, Mrs. Ator's fourth grade, Mrs. Yates' fourth grade, Miss White's seventh and eighth grades, Shirley Steele, and the first author's fifth and sixth grades—a hearty thank you for their candid feedback, which revealed important information for all teachers about narrative and expository text. Thank you to Marcia Allington and her sixth grade students, also from Orchard, who provided feedback and insight related to recommendations about gifted students. And finally, we thank Jeff Johnston, Naura Gillespie, and other Merrill editors for their continued support, thoroughness, and patience.

CONTENTS

FORM C

FORM S

FORM SS

FROM AUTHORS TO TEACHERS—
QUESTIONS AND ANSWERS

Why do teachers use an informal reading inventory?

"My first grader," the anxious mother proceeded, "reads from a fifth-grade book. He's been reading since he was 3. The kindergarten teacher allowed him to read with a volunteer, and also by himself in the reading corner. His father and I are anxious that his reading needs are met. The principal suggested that I talk with you. What do you plan to do about my child's reading program this year?"

"My fourth grader," a father confided, "has had difficulty reading since she started school. Can you tell me exactly what are her problems? What can we do to help her?"

"My sixth grader is always in the middle of the pack! She has been doing fine up to this point, but now she seems to be having some problems. Can you tell me about her major strengths and her shortcomings before she goes on to middle school?"

"I have a high school student who is a very capable learner, yet he still has difficulty reading. We don't exactly understand his problem . . ."

Regardless of their ages or grades, all types of readers are sitting in today's classrooms. They include talented children who are reading far ahead of the others, talented children who are experiencing difficulties, children who have had reading problems since the beginning of school, children who are encountering difficulties as the assignments become more complex, and children who are performing consistently in the average range. It is teachers who are held accountable for the analysis of the reading needs of the students in their classrooms, and also for an explanation of what will be done to facilitate learning. Because students' success in school depends upon their ability to cope with print, teachers should know as much as possible about how the students in their classrooms, reading labs, and gifted programs contend with written text.

An informal reading inventory is the evaluation instrument that reveals first-hand information about students' coping strategies as they read the kind of text used in the classroom. Such specific information as how students cope with material at the various levels of instruction, the strategies the reader uses to recognize words, and most important, the strategies used to understand the meaning of the text, is the kind of information revealed through IRI analyses. Without this information teachers cannot feel confident making everyday classroom decisions intended to provide meaningful instruction. Without this information we cannot provide effective communication for parents, other teachers, and school administrators concerning the nature of students' reading behaviors.

Can't teachers get the same information from another source?

No. Standardized testing is done in large groups. In contrast, an informal reading inventory is given in a one-to-one observation-and-response style. The informal setting provides a more relaxed and natural environment in which to gather data, hence one reason for the name *informal* reading inventory.

Standardized evaluation, often referred to as **formal data**, renders information not only about a student's performance, but also about that student's performance in relationship to that of other students. Informal analysis reflects information about how the student processes text, specifically the type of text that appears in the routine of the classroom day. This type of information, called **absolute data**, provides teachers with explicit knowledge that can be used to establish an instructional plan.

Since use of an informal reading inventory renders specific information about how the reader copes with print, the focus of informal diagnosis is on the reading process. Analysis of a reader's process, therefore, calls for an examiner to understand quantitative data that represent an overview of the reader's performance, and qualitative data that render specific information about how the reader copes with print. The strategies a reader uses to deal with print are what we refer to as **coping strategies**. The term **reading inventory** then becomes meaningful, as it refers to an inventory of coping strategies used by a reader to decode, and most importantly, to comprehend the material read each day at school. It is this type of specific information that teachers find valuable to support decisions about instruction.

Which students should be given the informal reading inventory?

It is important that teachers understand the coping strategies of all students—gifted, remedial, and all readers in between. The Analytical Reading Inventory (ARI) contains passages graded primer through ninth, and when deemed appropriate, can prove useful in determining information about students' coping strategies from kindergarten through high school.

When a teacher gives the Analytical Reading Inventory (ARI), what specific information about a reader's coping strategies can be learned?

The ARI is a convenient, efficient, and accurate guide for practicing teachers, as well as for university students enrolled in courses on diagnosis and correction of reading problems. The word *analytical* was selected because it means examining the component parts of the task of reading in relationship to the whole task. The ARI is designed to be used as an individual analysis enabling the teacher to discover what strategies each student employs when reading both narrative and expository text. The examiner can investigate the following components:

1. Identify a general level of word recognition
2. Identify strengths and weaknesses in word recognition strategies
3. Examine performance in oral and/or silent reading
4. Examine comprehension strategies through retellings and questions
5. Find the independent reading level
6. Find the instructional reading level

7. Find the frustration level
8. Find the reading capacity or listening level

What types of passages are included in the ARI?

The fourth edition of the ARI provides three forms—A, B, and C—of passages (narrative style), grades primer through nine. Narrative-style text is found in basal reading and literature books. It also includes content area passages (expository style), one form of science passages, grades one through nine, and one form of social studies passages, grades one through nine.

Does an examiner gather the same specific information about a reader's coping strategies from both narrative and expository text?

Using the ARI, an examiner gathers specific information about a reader's word recognition and comprehension coping strategies in both styles of text.

Since reading instruction in grades one through six is traditionally conducted by placing students in small groups and assigning material that is selected at the appropriate reading level, an examiner will give enough narrative passages from one ARI form to analyze a student's four reading levels—independent, instructional, frustration, and listening. This information will help teachers make sound decisions about grouping students.

However, in science and social studies classes, instruction is often conducted with the whole class reading from the same text. Therefore, it is recommended that an examiner analyze the students' level of performance at grade level only. This data will help a teacher to understand how the students as individuals and as a group cope with the text, and consequently will help the teacher make confident decisions about the most effective way to use the content area text.

Is there a difference between the way students cope with narrative text and the way they cope with expository text?

Yes, most certainly! Due to the fact that narrative and expository texts are structured differently, students may cope differently with each type. The authors of the ARI believe that it is important for teachers to analyze students' reading behaviors in both styles of text. Information that describes the two kinds of texts is included in the Development and Validation section beginning on page 9.

When should the ARI be given?

A teacher needs to have the information about students' coping strategies near the beginning of the school year. The information will help the teacher to determine placement in reading groups more effectively and to make sound decisions about how to conduct instruction.

Can the ARI be given more than once during the year?

Since additional forms of narrative passages are included, a teacher may periodically reevaluate to find out if a student's coping strategies are changing. Science or social studies reevaluation can periodically be done with the ARI or the student's own textbook.

Why is all of this important?

The essence of our job as teachers is to develop an understanding of how students cope with the academic requirements of our classrooms, to gain the specific knowledge of what can be done to facilitate our students' intellectual growth, to implement instruction based upon that knowledge, and, finally, to evaluate the effect of the instruction. The ability to perform this task with competence and expertise can bring dignity and pride to teachers. The good judgment and sound educational decisions that spring from this competence can serve as the foundation on which to build the respect and trust of the general public.

Mary Lynn Woods
Alden J. Moe

HOW TO USE THIS INVENTORY

For those individuals who intend to use this inventory for assessing the reading performance of students, it is recommended that the entire inventory be read carefully, including all graded passages, narrative and expository, and the comprehension questions. Since many individuals who use this inventory will be familiar with informal assessment procedures, the information listed below, concerning the contents of each major section, is presented to permit greater efficiency in using the inventory.

Organization

The organization of the word lists and passages to be used with the student is discussed in this section. Since inventories differ in their organization, this section is also recommended reading for all users of the inventory.

Development and Validation

All matters relating to the development and validation of the inventory are presented in this section. Specifically, the writing of the student passages, the development of the comprehension questions, the various analyses that were conducted on the passages to ensure continuity in readability, and the field testing with students are all presented in some detail. Also in this section is descriptive statistical information concerning the nature of the graded passages. This section is recommended reading for persons interested in readability and the computer assisted analysis of language. It is *not*, however, essential reading for all users of the inventory.

Instructions

Since this section deals specifically with the use of this inventory, a careful reading is recommended, even for those acquainted with the use of reading inventories.

Sample Student Record Summary Sheet
and Qualitative Analysis Summary Sheet

It is important for the user to read this section because the sample write-up demonstrates the extent and quality of information that can be known about a student's coping strategies through informal diagnosis.

Instructional Recommendations

This section gives the user a sampling of the kinds of decisions a teacher can make about classroom instruction.

Student Passages

It is imperative that users of this inventory read and become familiar with all passages, narrative and expository, before any of the passages are used with a student. It is also essential that the examiner carefully read the teacher's copies of the passages, the accompanying background information, and the comprehension questions before the passages are used for diagnosis.

Student and Class Record Summary Sheets

The use of the various summary sheets contained in this inventory is discussed under "Instructions."

References

The last section of the inventory contains three sets of references. The first set includes selected references on corrective and remedial reading instruction. The second set includes the references that have been cited in various sections of the inventory, and the last set includes the references that provided the background information necessary to write the student passages. While none of these three sets of references is essential, users of the inventory may find the first one of help in developing an instructional plan after the diagnosis.

There are five sections of the ARI that are to be used in assessing readers' coping strategies. Three sections consist of a series of graded word lists and a series of graded narrative passages (sometimes referred to as selections). With both the word lists and the narrative passages, there are student booklet copies and teacher record copies. The two expository sections consist of a series of graded social studies and science passages. A student copy and a teacher record copy are included in each section. The student will read from the student booklet, and the teacher will make notations concerning the reading on the teacher record forms or on a reproduced copy.[1]

There are seven word lists for each form, with each list containing twenty words. They are graded as follows:

> primer
> first grade
> second grade
> third grade
> fourth grade
> fifth grade
> sixth grade

For each of the three narrative forms, there are ten passages graded as follows:

> primer
> first grade
> second grade
> third grade
> fourth grade
> fifth grade
> sixth grade
> seventh grade
> eighth grade
> ninth grade

---

[1] Permission is granted by the publisher to reproduce the teacher record forms and the summary sheets.

The teacher may use any of the three forms (A, B, or C) since they are equivalent forms, and one may be used independently of the other two.

There are nine science passages graded as follows:

first grade
second grade
third grade
fourth grade
fifth grade
sixth grade
seventh grade
eighth grade
ninth grade

There are nine social studies passages graded as follows:

first grade
second grade
third grade
fourth grade
fifth grade
sixth grade
seventh grade
eighth grade
ninth grade

DEVELOPMENT AND VALIDATION

The development of the first edition of the Analytical Reading Inventory took place over a two-year period and included writing, field testing, computer analyses, and several revisions of the thirty originally written passages. With the inclusion of expository passages, similar procedures were followed for the preparation of the fourth edition. This section contains information concerning the content of all graded passages, the nature of the comprehension questions, the procedures used for establishing the readability and equivalency of forms for the narrative passages, progression of difficulty data for narrative and expository passages, and the field testing information with elementary and middle school students. Finally, this section includes discussions of the criteria used for the identification of the various reading levels for narrative passages, and the comprehension of the expository passages.

Passage Content

One of the objectives was to prepare original narrative writings that were motivational for both boys and girls and also nonsexist in nature. Therefore, a considerable amount of effort was expended learning about the reading interests of students at varying grade levels. Such sources as *Children and Books* (Arbuthnot & Sutherland 1972), *The New York Times Report on Teenage Reading Tastes and Habits* (Freiberger 1973), *Reading Interests of Children and Young Adults* (Kujoth 1970), and *Reading Children's Books and Our Pluralistic Society* (Tanyzer & Karl 1972) provided information that influenced the content and style of the selections in the ARI.

The situations depicted in the passages are actions and events corresponding to children's feelings so that the reader may perceive himself or herself in the situation, maintain empathy with the principal character in the selection, or be held by fascination of the mysterious. The passage topics were carefully selected to appeal to both boys and girls.

In addition, the content of the narrative passages is consistent across all three forms. For example, all passages at the sixth-grade level deal with famous scientists or inventors, who developed some lifesaving technique or device. Because both content, which affects the reader's motivational appeal, and readability are consistent, two major variables that influence a student's performance are controlled. This becomes a major factor in reassessment and also in the comparison of oral and silent reading comprehension.

Although the passages were not written with a controlled vocabulary, the careful selection of words had to be a factor in the creation of the passages. Therefore, word selection was guided in some cases by the graded word lists contained in *Basic Elementary Reading Vocabularies* (Harris & Jacobson 1972).

Because it was important that the passages reflect the writing style that students read in the science and social studies texts, both the selection and the writing of the expository passages were carefully reviewed.

The science passages, Levels four through nine, were selected from the science textbooks published by Merrill Publishing Company. Passages four through six are from *Accent on Science* (Sund et al. 1985); passages seven and eight from *Principles of Science*, 1986; and passage nine is from *Merrill General Science* (Moyer & Bishop 1986). Levels one, two, and three are original, yet represent topics that are included in the Merrill primary texts.

The social studies passages, Levels seven through nine, were selected from the social studies textbook, *America Is* (Drewery & O'Connor 1987), published by Merrill Publishing Company. Levels one through six are original, but represent topics that are included in published social studies textbooks.

Since the passages included in the ARI are intended for diagnosis rather than instruction, the selection of passages was based upon a list of considerations that relate to diagnostic intentions. The following list was generated for the selection of ARI passages:

1. A passage must be short with cohesive, meaningful content.
2. The level of each passage should increase in difficulty. The length of the passage, the concept load, the density of ideas, and the tendency of content area vocabulary to be polysyllabic are significant factors affecting readability of a text. In light of these factors, using a readability formula to reflect the difficulty of a passage would provide limited if not misleading data. For example, polysyllabic words affect the quantitative outcome of a formula. The words *America, explorations*, and *centuries*, cause the readability of Level Four to be quantitatively higher, when actually the vocabulary and the concepts are reasonable for that level. Furthermore, when the Level Eight passage about the Vietnamese War was read by sixth graders of varying reading abilities, all the students pronounced and understood the words *South Vietnamese, Communists*, and *guerrillas*, yet none was able to adequately retell the meaning of the passage. Therefore, instead of using a readability formula to demonstrate the increasing difficulty of the passages within the limited realm of quantitative information, data describing the number of total words, number of different words, vocabulary diversity scores, average sentence length, and longest sentence count were collected.
3. Because the purpose of the inventory is to analyze a student's coping strategies as he or she encounters print, the content of the passage must be meaningful without reliance on illustrations. Science or social studies instruction is often done by demonstration or illustration, and the lack of such aids has the potential of increasing the difficulty of the text. Therefore, the content of each passage was chosen with sensitivity to the background knowledge of readers.
4. All originally written passages, ones that did not come directly from a published textbook, must reflect the style of writing, the topics, and the vocabulary found in content area texts.

One of the major difficulties in the construction of informal reading inventories lies in devising questions that assess the reader's understanding of a passage. The prime concern in devising such questions is that they are passage dependent rather than experience based. The development of the questions was influenced by the work of Sanders (1966), Tuinman (1971), and Valmont (1972).

The questions used to measure comprehension in the ARI are of six types. They are listed with their abbreviations as follows:

1. Main idea (mi)
2. Factual (f)
3. Terminology (t)
4. Cause and effect (ce)
5. Inferential (inf)
6. Conclusion (con)

The first type of question, main idea (mi), was developed to ensure that the child derived the major focus of the passage. This question was designed either in an open-ended fashion revealing no facts or clues, or in a form where the reader was given *some* facts. The choice depended upon the complexity of the text.

The second type of question, factual (f), calls for facts that have been explicitly stated in the text. This type of question deals with only literal understanding.

The terminology (t) question is the only question that may or may not be completely text related. A terminology question may be text related because clues are given in the passage to aid the reader in deriving the meaning of the word or phrase. For example, the question, "What is meant by the word *challenger*?" is asked. The text states, "Look out, Sheila Young thought as she saw her challenger's bicycle come too close. At that moment a horrifying thing happened as she was bumped by another racer at forty miles an hour." In the second sentence a clue is given that will help the student derive the meaning of the word *challenger.*

On the other hand, in the text, "At dawn Jody awakened to the banging of the barn door," the question, "What is meant by the phrase *at dawn*?" is raised. In this sentence and the subsequent text there is no clue to the meaning of the phrase *at dawn.* This response requires the student to draw upon his or her background knowledge to demonstrate an understanding of the phrase.

Cause and effect questions (ce) require the reader to see relationships between facts given in the text. These questions are constructed so that the examiner provides either the cause or the effect, and the student is asked to supply the other.

Inferential (inf) questions require that the pupil infer a judgment or a deduction based on the facts stated in the text. In the ARI, an inferential question calls for the pupil to take *one* fact from the passage and deduct or infer his or her own conclusion. A conclusion (con) question requires that the pupil derive an answer from *two or more* facts stated in the passage. Thus, the distinction is made between these two types of questions.

Establishing the Reading Levels

Grade level validation of the reading level of each passage was established through the use of readability formulas and computer analyses of the text. The readability formulas provided grade level readability estimates for each of the passages, whereas the computer analyses provided specific information such as vocabulary diversity and syntactic complexity on the language used in each passage. Such procedures were used to assure that subsequent passages within a form increased in difficulty and also to assure that passages at a specific grade level were comparable among the three forms.

The revised Spache formula (Spache 1974) was used to calculate the readability estimates for passages at the primer through grade three levels, and the Harris-Jacobson Formula 2 (Harris & Sipay 1975) was used for levels four through nine. The readability estimates yielded by the Spache formula for the primary levels (primer through three) are summarized in Table I, and those yielded by the Harris-Jacobson formula for the intermediate grades and junior high (four through nine) are summarized in Table II. Since the Harris-Jacobson formula yields a predicted score which must be converted to a readability level, both the predicted score and the readability level are shown.

TABLE I

Spache readability results for primary narrative levels

Grade Level	Form A Score	Form B Score	Form C Score
Primer	1.5	1.5	1.5
One	1.7	1.7	1.8
Two	2.5	2.4	2.5
Three	3.2	3.4	3.1

TABLE II

Harris-Jacobson readability results for intermediate and junior high narrative levels

Grade Level	Form A		Form B		Form C	
	Predicted Score	Readability Level	Predicted Score	Readability Level	Predicted Score	Readability Level
four	4.78	four	4.73	four	4.63	four
five	5.61	six	4.85	five	4.98	five
six	6.07	seven[a]	5.79	seven[a]	6.27	seven[a]
seven	5.88	seven[a]	5.58	six	5.98	seven[a]
eight	7.44	eight +[a]	7.08	eight +[a]	8.29	eight +[a]
nine	7.78	eight +[a]	7.26	eight +[a]	8.02	eight +[a]

[a]Scores provided are based on extrapolation. See Harris and Sipay (1975) for further information.

Caution must be expressed to those who would conclude, on the basis of the information presented in Table II, that level six of Form A, for example, is more difficult than level seven. The results of readability formulas provide estimates; they are imprecise, but they do provide a gauge for comparing text.

Because a number of factors determine the extent to which a passage is or is not readable, additional analyses of the student passages were conducted. One of these analyses was an examination of the vocabulary diversity of each passage. Vocabulary diversity is the extent to which the vocabulary items, the words, differ within a text. For example, a 100-word passage written with 100 *different* words is more diverse than a 100-word passage written with only 20 *different* words. Factors used to compute a vocabulary diversity score for each passage—the total number of words and the number of different words contained in each passage—together with the vocabulary diversity scores are summarized in Table III.[2]

TABLE III

Number of total words, number of different words, and vocabulary diversity score for each narrative level of Forms A, B, and C

Level	Number of Total Words			Number of Different Words			Vocabulary Diversity Score		
	A	B	C	A	B	C	A	B	C
Primer	50	50	50	25	26	34	2.5	2.6	3.4
One	79	77	76	41	55	42	3.3	4.4	3.4
Two	118	113	118	71	77	78	4.6	5.1	5.1
Three	143	138	148	86	94	88	5.1	5.7	5.1
Four	144	157	144	96	96	87	5.7	5.4	5.1
Five	171	197	192	116	120	104	6.3	6.0	5.3
Six	192	186	189	115	123	117	5.9	6.4	6.0
Seven	262	235	240	148	150	145	6.5	6.9	6.6
Eight	286	283	257	170	179	172	7.1	7.5	7.6
Nine	339	321	315	200	190	197	7.7	7.5	7.8

The information presented in Table III shows that there is consistency within levels and that, generally, there is an increase in the length of the passages from one level to the next. There is also consistency with the number of different words contained in each passage within a grade level, and, in most cases, there is an increase as the grade level increases. The vocabulary diversity scores also show consistency within grade level, and with few exceptions there is an increase in the vocabulary diversity as the grade level increases.

TABLE IV

Number of total words, number of different words, and vocabulary diversity score for each level of the social studies and science forms

Level	Number of Total Words		Number of Different Words		Vocabulary Diversity Score	
	Social Studies	Science	Social Studies	Science	Social Studies	Science
One	80	83	40	45	3.2	3.5
Two	130	121	83	57	5.1	3.7
Three	156	140	90	59	5.1	3.5
Four	172	172	99	101	5.3	5.4
Five	190	200	100	109	5.1	5.5
Six	206	218	136	105	6.7	5.0
Seven	290	282	156	121	6.5	5.1
Eight	288	289	157	139	6.5	5.8
Nine	349	352	192	172	7.3	6.5

[2]The technical term for this score is **type-token ratio**. Because the passages varied in length, a corrected type-token ratio was calculated where the number of different words was divided by the square root of two times the total number of words.

Table IV provides information concerning the vocabularies used in the expository (social studies and science) passages. The information shows that there is an increase in the length of the passages and an increase in the number of different words used as the levels increase. The vocabulary diversity scores show that there is a general increase in the diversity as the grade level increases.

Another measure of the difficulty of text may be gained by examining sentence length. Although sentence length was a factor in determining the readability estimates, the average sentence length and the longest sentences contained within each passage are also presented as evidence that there is both grade level consistency *and* a progression of difficulty from levels primer through nine. Information on sentence length is summarized in Tables V and VI.

TABLE V

Average sentence length and longest sentence for narrative passages

	Average Sentence Length			Longest Sentence		
	A	B	C	A	B	C
Primer	6.3	6.3	6.3	8	9	11
One	8.8	8.6	8.4	13	11	11
Two	9.1	9.4	9.8	13	16	17
Three	11.9	11.5	12.3	25	20	21
Four	11.1	12.1	12.0	17	26	17
Five	13.2	16.4	16.0	24	34	27
Six	16.0	15.5	14.5	23	19	23
Seven	18.7	15.7	16.0	37	26	31
Eight	19.1	17.7	17.1	39	29	34
Nine	18.8	17.8	18.5	39	28	30

The figures presented in Table V show that the grade level increases as the average sentence length increases. Similarly, the longest sentence contained within a passage is *likely* to be longer as the grade level increases.

TABLE VI

Average sentence length and longest sentence for the social studies and science passages

	Average Sentence Length		Longest Sentence	
	Social Studies	Science	Social Studies	Science
One	10.0	9.2	12	16
Two	10.0	9.3	16	15
Three	11.1	7.8	16	16
Four	11.6	11.5	20	17
Five	13.6	8.7	21	19
Six	12.9	11.5	23	14
Seven	12.6	12.3	22	20
Eight	16.0	10.7	36	24
Nine	12.9	12.1	22	25

Table VI shows that the sentences for the science passages are shorter than those found in the narrative passages (forms A, B, and C) and in the social studies passages. The reason for these shorter sentences is that the writers chose to aid comprehensibility by decreasing syntactic complexity in passages where vocabulary difficulty was great. Hence, with a more difficult vocabulary, the sentences are shorter.

The information presented in Tables III and V should be used with and compared to the readability estimate figures presented in Tables I and II. The authors believe that the information from the tables along with the nonquantitative considerations support the conviction that the grade levels assigned to the narrative and expository passages are valid, and that among the three narrative forms there is consistency within the grade levels. In truth, the actual readability of a text is content related and the final test as to whether a passage can be read and understood is to have it read by those for whom it is intended. Therefore, extensive field testing with elementary and middle-school students was also undertaken.

Field Testing

A delineation of all the steps that led to the field testing of the narrative passages with students is difficult because at various stages in the development of the inventory some portions were partially tested and revised prior to the field testing. For example, if doubt arose concerning the content or the wording of a specific passage, it was "tried out" on school-age children. A similar procedure was used with the comprehension questions. Often the advice of classroom teachers and reading specialists was solicited when a particularly troublesome problem arose.

Finally, the ARI needed field testing by individuals unassociated with its development. This testing was accomplished by having approximately 80 advanced undergraduate students (in their second course on reading instruction) use it to assess the reading strategies of approximately 200 students in grades two through eight. The users of the inventory were asked to pay particular attention to (1) the appropriateness of the directions for its use, (2) the motivational appeal of the respective passages, (3) any ambiguities in the passages or the questions, and (4) the extent to which the comprehension questions were passage dependent.

Results of the field testing showed the major problem to be with the comprehension questions, and many were subsequently revised. Directions on how to make use of the results were also improved by including a qualitative summary sheet of student performance. Field testing also indicated that some passages were too difficult, and they were rewritten at an easier reading level. Finally, the passages and the questions were sent to Merrill Publishing for editing, and then the final readability checks and computer analyses of the text were conducted.

There is a great deal of evidence (Calfee & Curley 1984; Irwin 1986; Kent 1984; McGee & Richgels 1985; Meyer & Rice 1984; Piccolo 1987; Vacca & Vacca 1986) that indicates that narrative and expository texts are structured differently. Most students arrive at kindergarten with a basic understanding of story structure, causing the reading of story and literature material to be more comprehensible. The structure, however, of expository text is not as familiar, making it more difficult to understand and recall.

To demonstrate the distinction between the two styles of text, eighty-six students, grades two through eight at Orchard Country Day School in Indianapolis, Indiana, participated in a field study. The purpose of the study was to find out, for each grade level, which ARI passage—narrative (from Form C), science, or social studies—students felt was most difficult to comprehend and the reasons for the difficulty. For example, each fourth grader was given three unmarked fourth grade passages—a narrative, a science, and a social studies passage. Each student was asked to read all three passages and write a summary statement. Next, the student was to rank the three passages from easiest to hardest and explain why each was ranked in that position. Finally, to ensure that students understood the passages, oral discussions were conducted, comprehension questions were asked, and summary statements were checked.

Almost uniformly across grade levels two through eight, the narrative passages were ranked as the easiest, and the expository passages were ranked as the next easiest and hardest. Depending upon the reader's background knowledge and reading interests, the social studies and science passages interchanged positions between next easiest and hardest. It is interesting to note that most students intuitively sensed the different writing styles among the texts. Many referred to narrative text as "story" while the expository texts were often called "science or social studies facts." In six instances, a social studies or science passage was ranked as the easiest, but only in cases where the readers engaged in outside reading about the topics.

The outcome of this study tells us that students find expository text harder to read than narrative text. Without the framework of story schema, readers reported that they had to expend more mental energy interpreting and remembering the information in expository text. The common complaints centered on difficulty in recalling a series of details, and reading and understanding content area vocabulary. It was a sixth grader who so graphically described his feelings about the sixth grade social studies passage:

> After I read the first sentence, I had trouble getting the rest. Some-
> how I just kept forgetting the stuff. I had to stop and think at the
> end of each sentence, and then try to get it. It was like a mind twister!

Since this study was naturalistic, the student's comments about the passages proved to be very revealing information not only about the issue of narrative versus expository text, but also about what readers do as they read for meaning. The following are selected comments that help us to understand what thoughts travel the minds of student readers as they engage with text. The information in parentheses following each comment identifies the content of each passage.

Level	Narrative	Expository
2	This is like a story. (dog)	I didn't like to read this one. It was too hard. It was not like a story. (sound)
3	This kind of thing happens a lot in neighborhoods. It's like a story. (clubhouse)	This one is not as easy as the clubhouse. We have heard about Thomas Jefferson before though, and when you start to read about someone you know about your memory picks it up. (United States independence)

(continued)

Development and Validation

Level	Narrative	Expository
4	It's about a kid, his horse, and when his horse died. I have a pet. I can understand that. (pony)	The Jody story was the easiest. Really, it was hard for me to say which was the hardest. I love science! I read about it a lot. I saw all the stuff on TV about Halley's Comet. Wow! It was something! Well, I guess the Jody story was still easier to read. (comets)
		This one was about an explorer like in history. Everything about history is hard for me. It's really hard for kids to know about things way back in the 1600s! (La Salle)
5	I like stories about racing, and this is a story. (Muldowney)	When I read things that happened a long time ago I get all messed up! (slavery)
6	This story caught my attention because the human body is very interesting. I think about being a general surgeon. (heart surgery)	I didn't understand this one very well. But weaving thread, machines, and inventions just aren't important to me. That's just my opinion. (Industrial Revolution)
7	I think this story was sad. I have an older brother. I wanted the ending to be different. (drugs)	This one was in the middle because it was informational, and the writer explained it in such a way that it made it more understandable for me. (Vietnamese War)
	I think this one was the easiest because it was written in more of a story form, not so informational or with such big words. (drugs)	This one was too informational, and I found it to be the hardest. (inertia)
8	This one was the easiest because it flowed easily, and I could get a picture of what the author was saying. Sort of like a story. (Dracula)	I thought this one the next easiest to read because I'm interested in sports. Plus, when I read something new, the author explained what it was about and how it all tied together. (education)
		This one was the hardest to read because of all the big words. I don't know what all those words mean and so I totally lost what was happening. (cancer)

Criteria for Determining Narrative Levels

Since one of the functions of the ARI is to establish reading levels for narrative text, the criteria used for determining those levels become important. The criteria long used to establish the informal reading inventory levels have generally been attributed to Betts (Beldin 1970; Pikulski 1974). However, Powell (1970) and Powell and Dunkeld (1971) have suggested that the numerical standard used for determining the instructional level is too stringent, particularly at lower levels.

In an attempt to determine whether the Betts criteria or the Powell criteria were more appropriate, Pikulski (1974) reports contradictory findings. While users of the inventory should consider Powell's advice that the 95% word recognition score used for determining the instructional level may be too high for primary grade students, they should also realize that Ekwall (1976a, 1976b) presents strong evidence that Betts criteria should be maintained. Therefore, the criteria used to determine the three reading levels and the listening levels are those traditionally used and identified (the Betts criteria) in *Informal Reading Inventories* (Johnson & Kress 1965). These criteria are enumerated in detail on pages 12–19, and all scoring guides in the ARI are based on them.

Criteria for Teacher Judgment of Expository Passages

Expository style reading experiences are required in the daily routine of our classrooms; thus, it is extremely important that teachers understand how students contend with the content area texts. Since most content area instruction is conducted in a large group setting and most often with a grade level text, the questions which need answers are: (1) At what level—independent, instructional, or frustration—does the reader deal with the text? (2) What strategies is the student using as he or she functions at the determined level?

It is important for teachers to realize that most readers will have more difficulty reading expository text than they will reading narrative text. The following differences may be found: (1) the retelling of the expository passages may not be as complete as the narrative; (2) the reader may miscue more vocabulary words; and (3) the specific details of the comprehension questions may not be remembered as easily. If an examiner realizes this pattern of response may be typical, the reader's behaviors can then be better understood from a qualitative viewpoint. Careful and realistic judgment can then be exercised, so that sound instructional decisions can be made.

INSTRUCTIONS

Because the inventory is used to identify a reader's coping strategies and levels of reading achievement, it is necessary to have a systematic method of examining and recording the student's reading behaviors. The method most often used is to note the mispronunciations (referred to as **miscues**) as the student reads orally and to assess the student's comprehension immediately after the passage has been read. The following sections present discussions of: quantitative and qualitative analysis; passage comprehension, including retellings and the types of comprehension questions; the criteria for establishing each of the reading levels; oral reading; silent reading; diagnosis versus instruction; a step-by-step procedure for administering the ARI; and summarizing results.

Quantitative and Qualitative Analysis

Generally, users of informal reading inventories have relied upon a system of coding oral reading where all deviations from the text have been tabulated. This procedure has also been referred to as a quantitative analysis (Pikulski 1974), since deviations were simply counted and a score was computed. In recent years the word *miscue* has become popular (Goodman 1973; Goodman & Burke 1972). A miscue is defined as a deviation from the text. However, not all miscues occur consistently in a student's reading behavior or are indicative of a serious reading problem. For example, if a student substitutes the word *the* for *a*, indicating no change in the meaning of the text, the miscue is not as severe as the substitution of the word *read* for *think*. To best document patterns in a student's reading behavior, the examiner's major concern is to determine if the miscues occur consistently throughout a reading passage, and if they are the type of deviations that change the meaning of the text.

In order to obtain a comprehensive analysis, it becomes necessary to observe a student's reading behaviors from a qualitative as well as a quantitative viewpoint.[3] A qualitative viewpoint is gained by analyzing the reader's coping strategies within the context of the whole passage. An examiner must think about obtaining answers

---

[3]For those who wish a careful treatment of the distinctions between quantitative and qualitative analyses, see Goodman & Burke (1972).

to questions that will lead to a detailed understanding of the reader's process. Such questions are:

At what level does the reader look like the most confident, intelligent reader?

At what level does the reader begin to struggle?

At what level does the reader lose confidence and the control of effective strategies?

What types of miscues occur consistently at a given level or across levels?

Is the meaning of the text significantly altered? If so, why?

In this inventory two sheets have been provided for summarizing the information gained from observing a student's reading process. The completion of the Student Record Summary Sheet renders a quantitative overview, and the Qualitative Analysis Summary Sheet provides the opportunity for the examiner to understand the specific nature of the reader's miscues within the context of a passage.

Passage Comprehension

Retellings

After a student has read a passage, the examiner wants to know how thoroughly the passage was understood. It is recommended that before asking the comprehension questions, the examiner require the reader to retell the passage. A comprehensive retelling gives information about the characters, the setting, and the schematic structure of the plot. A retelling provides the necessary information an examiner needs to determine the adequacy of the reader's comprehension. Insight can also be gained about the reader's use of language in relationship to the author's language. It should be remembered that a retelling of expository passages may be less thorough than that of narrative passages.

Directions for administering and evaluating a retelling and recommendations for giving and scoring comprehension questions are found in this section, page 24, Step 4.

Comprehension Questions

A definition of each of the types of comprehension questions and the rationale for the use of each were discussed previously. However, the major concern in the development of the questions for each passage was that they be passage dependent; that is, the successful answering of a comprehension question should be based upon information gained from reading the passage rather than based upon information the student had acquired from previous experiences. With the exception of some of the terminology questions, it is felt that comprehension questions for the ARI are passage dependent.[4]

The following types of comprehension questions are included in the ARI (see p. 11 for a detailed description):

---

[4]Anderson (1977) provides further verification of the passage dependency of the comprehension questions.

1. Main idea (mi)
2. Factual (f)
3. Terminology (t)
4. Cause and effect (ce)
5. Inferential (inf)
6. Conclusions (con)

When a student answers a question incompletely or inaccurately, the examiner must try to determine if there is some kind of pattern to the student's response. For example, some students may be able to answer the factual and terminology questions well but may have difficulty with the inferential and conclusion questions. Such an observation by the teacher has important implications for instruction.

Reading Levels

The reading behaviors associated with each reading level and a means of assessing oral reading are presented in the following sections.

Independent Level

This is the level at which the student can read with no more than one uncorrected miscue in each 100 words (99%) and with at least 90% comprehension. In some cases, the students reading at this level *may exceed* the above criterion for miscues if comprehension is maintained at the 90% level or higher. At the independent level, the student's reading is fluent and expressive with accurate observation of punctuation; the student recognizes the print with confidence.

Instructional Level

This is the level at which the student can read no more than five uncorrected miscues in 100 words (95%) and with at least 75% comprehension. In some cases, at this level, the student's reading may exceed the above criterion for miscues if comprehension is maintained at a higher level. At the instructional level, the student's reading is generally expressive though he or she reads more slowly than at the independent level.

Frustration Level

This is the level beyond which reading has little meaning. It may be thought of as the "breakdown point." Miscues exceed 10% (less than 90% correct) with comprehension about 50%. At this level, the student exhibits obvious frustration because the material is too difficult. Except for an occasional brief testing period, no child should be expected to read at this level.

Listening Level

This level is sometimes referred to as the hearing comprehension level, the hearing capacity level, or the reading potential level. It is the level at which the student can comprehend 75% of the materials read aloud by the examiner. This level provides an estimate of the child's reading potential and becomes important when it is compared with the instructional level.

Oral Reading

It is important to learn as much as possible about the student's knowledge of vocabulary, word recognition strategies, and inefficient reading habits as the student reads orally. The examiner should be recording all deviations from the text. The kinds of miscues that should be observed and a method of recording them is presented in Table VIII.

TABLE VIII

Type of Deviation from the Text	Recorded Example
Omission: Circle the word or punctuation mark omitted.	Jack lost his (brother's) bike.
Insertions: Write the inserted word or words.	Mary was not $\overset{very}{\wedge}$ happy.
Substitutions: Write the word substituted.	$\overset{house}{\text{The horse}}$ trotted along the road.
Aided Words: Draw a line through the word pronounced for the student. (An examiner should aid words for a reader as seldom as possible.)	Mark began to tremble.
Repetitions: Record only if two or more words are repeated.	Chris is serious about her career.
Reversals: Use curved lines to indicate words or letters reversed.	He lay exhausted on the ground.
Hesitation: Use a slash (/) to denote improper hesitation. Do not count as miscues.	That was no/laughing matter.

If a student makes a miscue or some other deviation from the text but self-corrects, it should be recorded as self-correction (SC). A self-correction should *not* be a counted miscue. It should be noted that a reader who self-corrects is one who is monitoring the meaning, and the miscues should be recorded on the Qualitative Analysis Summary Sheet. Some examples of recorded self-corrections follow:

$$\overset{SC}{\underset{boys}{}}$$
An old beaver dam from upstream broke.

$$\overset{SC}{}$$
No one could enter (the tunnel.)

Silent Reading

There are some students who will comprehend a passage better when they read silently rather than orally. If the examiner feels the student should read a passage silently, alternate forms are provided in which selections of equivalent levels may be used. Examiner judgment in this situation might be based upon the following:

1. The reader is self-conscious and not relaxed when reading aloud.
2. The reader's major word recognition miscues are repetitions, and the examiner feels that a silent reading passage may render a more accurate analysis of the student's comprehension strategies.

Using the Inventory with a Student

Diagnosis Versus Instruction

Knowing the distinction between the purposes of diagnosis and the purposes of instruction helps to clarify the basic function of informal diagnosis. It is important to understand this distinction because it helps an examiner know how to respond during the diagnostic process.

The purpose of informal diagnosis is to gain an understanding of how the student deals with print. In order to best accomplish this, the examiner must behave as an observer and analyst. Therefore, the reader must perform as independently as possible with little or no assistance from the examiner. During diagnosis the student reads the text only once. Then, without referring to the text, the reader responds by retelling the passage and answering comprehension questions. In essence, an examiner is seeking an answer to this question: "If I were not here to facilitate the understanding of this text, what coping strategies would the reader be using to comprehend it?"

In contrast, the purpose of instruction is to facilitate a student's understanding of the text; thus, teacher behaviors are quite different. For example, as a student reads, a teacher may provide instruction that facilitates comprehension. After a text is read, common procedures include: rereading to clarify information; discussing; referring to other texts, illustrations, graphs, or visuals; and/or answering questions.

Diagnosis is a process of data gathering from which the examiner learns about the strategies used by the reader. In this process, examiner behaviors become a vital part of an accurate diagnostic outcome. A noted advantage held by informal diagnosis over other forms of diagnosis is that it is conducted in an informal, caring, personalized environment. An informal, relaxed atmosphere has the potential for fostering trust. If the examiner and student do not know each other, time should be spent to establish rapport. Because the examiner acts as observer and analyst, it is important to know that oral cueing and body language can affect the outcome of the evaluation. An examiner who is calm and quiet, who waits patiently for the reader to respond, will achieve more accurate results. It is recommended that the examiner tell the student that brief notes will be taken during the administration of the inventory. Many users of the inventory will find it valuable to tape record the entire session, enabling them to verify notations at a later time. If the tape recorder is used, it should not hamper the student's performance. Its use should be planned and the operation nondistracting. The following steps suggest the sequence to be used with both narrative and expository text.

Narrative Text

Step 1

Have the student begin reading the words in the primer isolated word list from the form you have selected. As the student says each word, note the pronunciation and record appropriately on the teacher record form. Mark a plus (+) if the word is pronounced correctly. If the word is incorrectly pronounced, write the word the student said. If the student did not know the word, mark DK, and if the student self-corrects a miscue, mark SC next to the word corrected.

Continue until the student misses (mispronounces or does not know) five of the twenty words in a list. In any list, stop at the point where the fifth word is missed unless the student expresses a strong desire to finish the list.

After the student has completed reading several lists, it is suggested that the examiner ask the student to use some randomly selected words from a list in a complete sentence. For example, the examiner might say, "Place number fifteen from list three in a sentence." It is also suggested that these sentences be written down on the corresponding teacher's record. This procedure will help the examiner to readily identify a student who might be a "word caller" (one who pronounces words correctly, but who has no concept of the meaning or knowledge of its proper use in context). Also, the procedure will facilitate the selection of the appropriate reading passage.

The next step, the oral reading, should be started at the highest level at which the student correctly pronounced all twenty words on a list. In some instances, where only one word was mispronounced, for example, the examiner may decide to start at a higher level. However, if in doubt as to where to start the oral reading, begin at the lower level.

Step 2

Open the booklet to a student narrative passage corresponding to the highest level at which the child successfully pronounced all words and used appropriately in context selected words from the word list.

It is recommended that the evaluator read carefully all examiner's introductions, passages, and questions prior to the administration of the ARI to ensure complete familiarity with the inventory. Most of the examiner's introductions are included to provide the evaluator with the necessary background for the passage. It is suggested that as little cueing as possible be given to the student prior to the reading of the narrative texts; therefore, most examiner's introductions need not be read to the student. However, if the evaluator feels that the student may be confused while reading the passage without some sort of an introduction, it is appropriate to include one. For example, the examiner might say: "Please read the following story. It is about something that happened many years ago. Sometimes, a long time ago, a school teacher might live with a student's family."

Step 3

Explain to the student that he or she will be doing some reading. Sometimes the reading material is called stories, sometimes it is called passages, and sometimes it is called text. Talk to the student about the meaning of these words, to ensure they are understood. Before the student begins to read, tell him or her that after the passage is read, you will ask for a retelling and possibly some comprehension questions. As the student reads from the student passage, record oral reading miscues on the corresponding teacher's passage. After the student has read aloud, take the booklet from the reader before assessing the comprehension.

Step 4

After the passage has been read ask the reader to retell the text. The examiner should record the retelling in the space provided on the Teacher Record Sheet.

Some examiners employ the time-saving convenience of the computer, using word processing software and typing as the student retells the passage. A complete retelling will include:

1. A listing of the characters, a description of the characters, or both
2. Reference to the time and setting of the passage, if applicable
3. A description of the plot or events told according to the author's sequence and logic
4. A summarization of the main idea

After the reader has told all that he or she intends to tell, the examiner may probe for further information. As a final probe to determine the reader's ability to summarize the main ideas, the examiner should say, "In one or two short sentences, tell me what this passage is about."

If a retelling is thorough, the examiner may choose not to ask any of the comprehension questions, or just select a few, such as vocabulary or another type for further probing. In the event of a thorough retelling, the comprehension score should be counted independent or instructional, depending upon the accuracy of the retelling and responses to the questions.

An example of thorough retelling follows. This is John's retelling of Level 2; Form C. (Note the passage found in the Teacher Record on page 135. Also see the Student Record Summary Sheet, page 30; the Qualitative Analysis Summary Sheet, pages 31–32; and the Description of Reading Behaviors, pages 33–35 for the write-up of John's reading performance.)

Retelling: This is story about a dog. The boy in the story yells to his dog, "Look out, you're gonna get hit!" The dog is running across a busy street. The dog gets hit anyway. The boy really feels bad. He almost starts to cry. He runs home to tell his mom and dad that his dog got hit. Someone has to help out. (See sample write-up on page 33.)

Examiner
Probe (Mi):   In one or two short sentences, tell me what this story is about.

Student
Response: It's about a dog that got hit in the street.

Examiner
Probe: Do you know the name of the dog?

Student
Response: Shēp

If a retelling is incomplete, the examiner should probe the reader by saying, "Can you tell me more?" An example of an incomplete retelling follows. This is John's retelling of Level 4, Form C on page 121. See pages 33–35 for the final analysis of John's reading performance.

Retelling: It's about a horse. Jody is real worried about the horse. It's sick. The wind blew the barn door open. It started banging.

Examiner
Probe: Can you tell me more?

Student
Response: That night Jody stayed with the horse. The alarm went off and Jody
                 saw something buzz around. The horse was gone.

Examiner
Probe: Can you tell me more?

Student
Response: No response

Examiner
Probe (Mi):   In one or two short sentences, tell what this story is about.

Student
Response: It's about a sick horse. The boy is worried.

When a reader responds to the comprehension questions, he or she may not
give the exact responses listed as possible answers in the teacher record. The
examiner must exercise personal judgment in determining what is an acceptable
response. For example, consider the responses to these questions from John's
evaluation, Level 4, Form C.

#3   Why did Jody take a blanket from the house? (so he could sleep near
                 Gabilan)

Student
Response: He wanted to stay all night in the barn with his sick horse.

#7   How did Jody try to find his pony? (He followed the pony's tracks.)

Student
Response: He ran through the banging barn door.

Examiner
Probe: How did Jody know where to look for his pony?

Student
Response: The door was open. The horse was gone.

#8   What is said in the story that makes you think Jody feared his pony
                 might be dead? (stated: Looking upward he saw buzzards, the birds
                 of death, flying overhead.)

Student
Response: He ran out of the barn.

Examiner
Probe: Do you remember anything that told you that he thought the pony
                 might be dead?

Student
Response: No response

Even though the response to question #3 is not the exact words of the
suggested response, the examiner determines that John understands why Jody
took the blanket to the barn. In question #7, however, even after probing, John
really doesn't know that Jody followed the pony's tracks. And with question #8,

John doesn't understand the implication found in the text. Examiner judgment, plus additional probing, must be exercised to determine if the student is actually deriving the correct meaning from the text.

Step 5

On the scoring guide at the bottom of the page, circle the appropriate level for both word recognition and comprehension. Sometimes an examiner finds that the miscue count either exceeds or falls short of the range indicated on the scoring guide. In this case a judgment must be made.[5] When determining a student's reading level, keep in mind that comprehension rather than word recognition is the ultimate goal. Some examples based upon the following scoring guide will help to clarify the matter.

Scoring Guide	
Word Rec.	Comp.
IND 1–2	IND 0
INST 7–8	INST 2
FRUST 15+	FRUST 4+

If the student made five word recognition miscues, produced a thorough retelling, and made zero comprehension mistakes, the level, in most instances, would be determined independent. After a quick assessment to ensure that the five word recognition miscues have not interfered with comprehension accuracy, the examiner would feel assured of a proper decision. If the student made seven word recognition miscues, produced an incomplete retelling, and made seven comprehension mistakes, the level would be frustration. If the student made ten word recognition miscues, produced a mediocre retelling, and made three comprehension mistakes, the level might be low instructional or frustration. A careful look at the severity of the miscues and the overt demeanor of the student would be necessary before a final judgment could be made. If, for example, the word recognition miscues appeared to have little effect on comprehension accuracy and if the student showed no signs of anxiety, then the level would be considered low instructional. However, if there were apparent signs of anxiety during the reading of the passage, and if the miscues severely interfered with comprehension accuracy, then the level would be considered frustration.

If the frustration level has not been reached, have the student read the next passage. After the frustration level has been reached, the student no longer reads. It is then necessary to identify the student's listening level. The listening level is determined by having the examiner read passages to the student. The examiner may choose to read the selection immediately after the passage found to be the reader's frustration level, or choose passages from another form if the examiner wishes to gather information from lower levels.

Step 6

Tell the student that you will read a passage aloud. Ask the student to listen carefully since he will be responsible for retelling the passage and answering some comprehension questions. Stop after the level at which the student comprehends

---

[5]This matter is thoroughly discussed in "Informal Reading Inventories: The Instructional Level" by Eldon E. Ekwall from *The Reading Teacher*, April 1976, *29*, 662–65.

75% of the material read aloud. On the scoring guide, this is the same as the instructional level.

Expository Text

Step 7

Because students seem to have more difficulty with the expository text, it is important that the examiner's introduction be used. This small piece of information will alert the student to the fact that he/she will be reading about a topic that is historical or scientific in nature. The examiner should tell the student that he/she will not be reading storylike passages, but rather science or social studies text.

Ask the student to read the science text at grade level. Follow the same procedure for coding the oral reading, the retelling, and the responses to the comprehension questions used with the narrative passages. Repeat the same method for the social studies text.

When evaluating the retelling and the responses to the comprehension questions, examiner judgment must be exercised. A retelling may not be as complete as retellings of the narrative passages, and responses to questions may not be as easily recalled. Sometimes responses may vary from the suggested response, yet a student may still have a reasonable answer based upon information from the text.

Step 8

Have the student return to class; then summarize the information discussed in the next section.

Since the successful use of the ARI requires familiarity with informal reading inventory procedures, and since some of the decision making is based upon subjective evaluations, it is recommended that users of this inventory practice its administration sufficiently so that they will thoroughly understand the procedures, the content of the passages, and the nature of the questions before using the inventory.

Summarizing the Results

Several ways of helping the examiner summarize the results of the student's performance are provided in this inventory. At the bottom of the teacher's copy is a space for tallying the oral reading miscues. There is also a Student Record Summary Sheet on which the results of the diagnosis are to be summarized. This sheet gives the user a quantitative overview of the student's progress. To get a detailed picture of the student's coping strategies and an analysis of the strength of the strategies at various levels, the Qualitative Analysis Summary Sheet should be used. This analysis affords perspective from the level at which the reader appears to be the most competent to the level at which he/she no longer deals successfully with the text.

Beginning on page 30 is a sample analysis of a fourth grade student demonstrating the extent of information that can be derived from informal diagnosis. Included are both quantitative and qualitative summary sheets and a descriptive write-up that logically evolved from the qualitative analysis. A section called Recommendations for Instruction follows the descriptive write-up. The recommendations are intended for use with individual students, small groups of students, or parents who wish to provide support at home. All sources for the recommendations are cited in the section of References on page 207.

Finally, there is a Class Record Summary Sheet on page 205. The sheet contains spaces for summarizing results of twelve students, showing the results of three separate administrations of the inventory.

SAMPLE STUDENT RECORD SUMMARY SHEETS AND DESCRIPTIVE ANALYSIS

STUDENT RECORD SUMMARY SHEET

Student __John Stone__ Grade __4__ Sex __M__ Age __9 - 10__
yrs. mos.

School __Merrill Elementary__ Administered by __M. L. Woods__ Date __1/18/88__

Grade	Word Lists	Graded Passages			Estimated Levels	
	% of words correct	WR Form _C_	Comp. Form _C_	Listen. Form _B_	Narrative	
Primer	100%					Grade
1	100%	⁻1 Ind.	⁻0 Ind.		Independent	1-2
2	100%	⁻3 Inst.	⁻2 Inst.		Instructional	2-3
3	95%	⁻7 Inst.	⁻3 Inst.	Inst.	Frustration	4
4	60%	⁻11 Inst.	⁻5 Frust.	Inst.	Listening	5
5		⁻18 Frust.	⁻6 Frust.	Inst.	Expository	
6				Frust.	Grade Level	
7					Science	Social Studies
8						
9						

Expository detail:

Science		Social Studies	
WR	Comp.	WR	Comp.
-1	-4	-11	-4
Frust.	Frust.	Frust.	Frust.

Check consistent oral reading difficulties:

____ word-by-word reading
____ omissions
____ substitutions ← (makes numerous word guesses)
____ corrections
____ repetitions
____ reversals
____ inattention to punctuation
____ word inserts
____ requests word help

Check consistent word recognition difficulties:

____ single consonants
____ consonant clusters
✓ long vowels } medial
✓ short vowels }
____ vowel digraphs
____ diphthongs
____ syllabication
✓ use of context (must strengthen)
____ basic sight
✓ grade level sight

Check consistent comprehension difficulties:

____ main idea
____ factual
✓ terminology
✓ cause and effect
✓ inferential
✓ drawing conclusions
✓ retelling

30

QUALITATIVE ANALYSIS SUMMARY SHEET

FORM __C__

Level	# of Miscues	STUDENT: John Stone / MISCUE IN CONTEXT	Meaning Change	DATE: 1/18/88 / NATURE OF MISCUE
2	②	"Look out, ~~you'll~~ [you're] get hit!"	yes	final substitution – used wrong sight word – no self-correction
		"Thud!" was the noise I heard, then I saw my pup ~~lying~~ [down] in the street.	no	whole word substitution meaning based
		"Mom! Dad!" I yelled as I ran ~~straight~~ [street ⓢⒸ] home.	SC	reader is self-correcting to insure meaning
		But they started rolling down my face anyway as I blasted ~~through~~ [thought ⓢⒸ] the door.	SC	reader is self-correcting to insure meaning
3	⑦	These are the signs which Jack ~~read~~ [reed] ...	yes	medial vowel – possible tense change no self-correction
		Jack was the new boy and he really wanted to ~~belong~~ [become] to the club.	yes	medial/final substitution no self-correction
		~~Suddenly~~ [Sunday] he dashed home and returned with a bucket...	yes	medial/final substitution no self-correction
		He began ~~pounding~~ [banging] on the clubhouse door.	no	whole word substitution no self-correction
		"I don't know the secret word," he said ~~remarked~~, "but...	no	whole word substitution no self-correction
		~~All~~ [And] the kids thought this was a great idea and quickly ~~invited~~ [invented] Jack to belong!	? yes	whole word sub. – no SC medial vowel – no SC
4	⑬	Jody was so worried that he didn't ~~even~~ [ever] care to eat.	yes	final substitution – no SC
		He had stayed in the barn all day to take care of his sick ~~pony~~ [pond], Gabilan Ⓐ.	yes no	final sub. – no SC no attempt
		The ~~pony's~~ [ponds ⓢⒸ] ~~condition~~ [con-di-ted] was growing worse.	SC yes	now reader knows word is pony SC with other miscue in mind medial/final sub. – no SC
		As his ~~breathing~~ [breath] grew louder and harder...	yes	slight meaning change final omission
		At nightfall Jody brought a blanket from the ~~house~~ [horse] so he could sleep...	yes	medial/final sub. Reader is confused about meaning
		In the middle of the night the wind ~~whipped~~ [blew] around the barn and blew the door open.	no	whole word sub. – probably saw "blew" on next line
		At dawn Jody ~~awakened~~ [awaked]...	?	medial omission – no SC
		In ~~alarm~~ [alone] he ran from the barn ~~following~~ [folding] his pony's tracks.	yes yes	medial/final sub. – no SC medial/final sub. – no SC

If additional space is needed, permission is granted by the publisher to reproduce this summary sheet.

FORM_____C_____

Level	# of Miscues	STUDENT: _John Stone_	Meaning Change	DATE: 1/18/88
		MISCUE IN CONTEXT		NATURE OF MISCUE
		Looking upward he saw ~~buzzards~~ ^{buzzes} _, the birds of death, flying overhead._	yes	final sub. - no SC
		_In a_ ~~clearing~~ ^{cloud} _below, he saw something that filled his heart with_ ~~anger~~ ^{ager} _..._	yes / yes	final sub. - no SC / medial sub. - no SC
5	-18	** _Miscues continued in the same pattern as at Level 4. They increased in number, consequently causing greater loss of comprehension. John now shows obvious signs of frustration._		
		*** 1/19/88 Science & Social Studies passages		
S	-12	_A long time ago people became_ ~~frightened~~ ^{fright} _when they saw..._	yes	final omission - no SC
		They thought a comet was a sign that ~~unpleasant~~ ^{unpleased} _..._	yes	medial / final sub. - no SC
		A comet is an object made of ~~particles~~ ^{parts} _mixed with..._	yes	final sub. - slight meaning change
		Comets ~~probably~~ ^{probe} _come from the far outer_ ~~edge~~ ^{age} _of our solar..._	yes / yes	medial / final sub. - no SC / initial sub. - no SC
		Comets can be seen only when they are close (~~enough~~) _to the_	yes	omission - no SC
		sun to ~~reflect~~ ^{refleat} _its light._	yes	medial vowel - no SC
		** _Miscues follow the same pattern as in narrative Level 4 – no self-correcting – even though John has some background knowledge about comets, meaning and retention are severely affected_		
SS	-11	** _Similar type miscues as in Science and narrative levels - no self-correcting - shows obvious signs of frustration._		

If additional space is needed, permission is granted by the publisher to reproduce this summary sheet.

DESCRIPTION OF READING BEHAVIORS—NARRATIVE AND EXPOSITORY
Narrative Reading Levels 2 and 3

Word Recognition. As John read Levels 2 and 3, I could tell that he expected to gain meaning from his reading. For example, he self-corrected many of the miscues demonstrating that he was using context clues to get meaning from the text as well as recognize words. At Level 3 he made some word substitutions that were appropriate for the meaning of the text (*banging* for *pounding, said* for *declared*), which showed that he was reading for meaning. At Level 3 he pronounced a previously miscued word correctly when it appeared later in the text, thus verifying that he was continuously searching for meaning (*become* for *belong*, but later corrected). John's most productive word pronunciation strategy was the use of initial consonants and some blends. Throughout both levels he had difficulty coping with the medial and final portions of the words. Although not an overriding problem at Level 3, uncorrected miscues did affect the meaning of the text (*read* for *read, Sunday* for *suddenly*). I am concerned that as the material becomes more complicated, the meaningful substitution strategy may not prove effective.

Comprehension. The retellings at Levels 2 and 3 contained adequate information about the passages. Both retellings showed that John thoroughly understood the sequence of events. Despite the fact that the number of miscues increased at Level 3, John's effort to read for meaning coupled with his background vocabulary demonstrated that he effectively coped at this level. After the retelling, I chose to ask all the comprehension questions to see if he had understood specific information. He responded appropriately in all instances.

Attitude. John appeared to be an intelligent, competent reader at Levels 2 and 3. Throughout the reading of both passages I could see that he was attempting to make meaning of the text. He appeared confident and self-assured as he read aloud, often subvocalizing the meaning as if he were constructing the parts of a puzzle. In summary, he coped adequately with the comprehension, and used effective word recognition strategies, causing Level 3 to be instructional.

Narrative Reading Level 4

Word Recognition. The number of miscues substantially increased at Level 4. The strategy of using the initial consonants and blends continued to be the more reliant cueing system. Difficulties persisted in the medial and final portions of the words. I could tell that his confidence was threatened because he often either waited for me to aid the word (*Gabilan*) or made a nonmeaningful whole-word substitution (*alone* for *alarm*) with no attempt to self-correct. He often glided by punctuation marks indicating that he was not grouping the author's ideas effectively. These behaviors indicate less effective coping strategies with this level of material.

Comprehension. John's retelling at Level 4 was scanty. It was randomly organized, never revealing the logic of the passage. Although John did concisely retell the main idea, when answering comprehension questions he not only had difficulty recalling some of the factual information, but also consistently missed questions requiring him to correlate portions of the text (ce) or to draw inferences from the text (inf/con). His description of many of the vocabulary words revealed their meanings, yet during the oral reading he had miscued some of them. His ability to use context clues at this level was not as effective as it had appeared at the previous level. A silent reading of Level 4, Form B rendered the same comprehension weaknesses.

Attitude. John did not look like or sound like the confident strategist he was at Level 3. He showed physical signs of stress, appearing less confident and more confused. He was reluctant to take as many risks as he had in Level 3, indicating that the coping strategies he had been using were not working as effectively.

Narrative Reading Level 5

Word Recognition/Comprehension/Attitude.   John's coping strategies seemed to fall apart at this level. He made so many oral miscues that he was unable to understand most of the text. He showed obvious signs of frustration and defeat.

Listening Level (Narrative)

When I read Level 4 from Form A, John's retelling was well organized and thorough. Level 5 showed some of the same qualities, but was not as thorough as Level 4. Answering the comprehension questions I used to further probe his understanding, he again demonstrated that he clearly understood the text. In both instances, his background knowledge of vocabulary strengthened his ability to understand. The quantity of information and vocabulary at Level 6 caused John to demonstrate frustration similar to his frustration in the oral Level 4 sample. This information confirms the fact that John can comprehend slightly more challenging material when he does not have to struggle with the recognition of the words. This information should prove useful in the selection of material that is read in class, and in determining expectations for his participation.

Recommendations for Instruction (Narrative).   John should start the year at a level where he appears to be the most intelligent strategist, confident and relaxed. I recommend that he be placed in the third grade, second semester basal (3/2). Many additional independent reading experiences using trade books as well as the basal should be provided. Instructional strategies designed to help him learn more effective coping strategies in word recognition, vocabulary development, and comprehension should be provided. John should soon be challenged with grade level material. (See Instructional Recommendations, page 36.)

Science Level 4

Word Recognition.   In expository text, the same miscue patterns occurred as in narrative text. The medial and final portions of words were most often missed. Very little self-correcting took place, which indicated that John was struggling so hard with the recognition of words and the organization of the text that he was unable to monitor the meaning successfully as he had done in narrative Levels 2 and 3.

Comprehension.   Even though he had some background knowledge about comets, he still had difficulty understanding the text. The effort he had to expend to recognize the words and process the text seemed to overpower his ability to get the meaning.

Attitude.   John was obviously frustrated. Even though this was the first reading on the second day of evaluation, he yawned, wiggled around in his seat, and often glanced up to see the clock.

Social Studies Level 4

Word Recognition.   The miscues followed the same pattern as found in the science and narrative Level 4 passages.

Comprehension.   Much energy was spent on word recognition and processing the text at the cost of meaning.

Attitude.   Even though John was trying very hard, he really had difficulty sticking to the task. He told me that it was hard to remember things that happened a long time ago and that maybe his grandmother would know more about it. He was truly frustrated.

Recommendations for Instruction (Expository).   Dealing with content area text is very challenging for John. Since over half of the class experienced similar difficulties, a plan for effective instruction will include:

Sample Student Record Summary Sheets and Descriptive Analysis

1. Providing reading experiences in alternate texts and other reading materials on each topic covered in both the science and social studies books. Films, filmstrips, and other visuals will be included. Materials should be at various levels of comprehension.
2. An instructional format that offers time for small group reading and discussion in the regular and alternate texts as well as whole group reading experiences.
3. Pairing students as reading and discussion partners when the content area text is used.
4. Instructional strategies that involve the student in predicting and analyzing possibilities of both concepts and vocabulary in the content area and alternate texts.
5. Advance organizers, both teacher- and student-made, which provide information about each reading assignment; thus, as units or chapters are introduced, students gain background experience with the content.
6. Weekly free reading time in which the teacher reads text to the students about the topics covered in the science and social studies texts, or students read and discuss the text and/or alternate texts.

INSTRUCTIONAL RECOMMENDATIONS

Word Recognition

Substitutions, Word Guesses, Context Clues,
Grade Level Sight Vocabulary/Content Area Vocabulary

It should be noted that if a reader is to attain comprehension of a particular written context, the vocabulary should always be held in its contextual framework. If word recognition practice is conducted, the isolation of words is not as beneficial to the reader as is recognition in context; therefore, all recommendations that follow should be considered only if the reader is offered the benefit of using the vocabulary in a meaningful context.

1. As the student reads and miscues a word, the teacher, tutor, or parent should provide a synonym or meaning-based phrase for the miscue. The reader should respond with the exact pronunciation of the word, or with a meaningful substitute. This strategy encourages the reader to attend to the meaning of the text, to maintain the flow and pace of the reading, and to maximize the use of context clues.[6]
2. Place sight words, basal vocabulary, and content area vocabulary words on individual cards to be used as study cards. The cards should be kept in a classroom, specific reading group or individual file, and should be continuously updated. Laminate sheets of lined paper (regular or primary). As file words are introduced to or miscued by the reader, the reader should be asked to write (on the laminated sheets with a marker) sentences or mini-stories using the words. The teacher, parent, or tutor should likewise write sentences or mini-stories on his/her sheet. Examples of a sentence and a mini-story are found on p. 39, #14, Context Clues. Sentences and stories can be shared within the group or between individuals. The sheets can then be wiped off, preparing them for reuse. This same strategy can also be done using overhead transparencies, markers, and projector.

---

[6]Adapted from Goodman, Burke, & Sherman (1981), p. 194.

3. Ask questions about the subject matter that will reflect the student's miscue. Have the student find the word in the text and reread the context.
4. Have the reader reread several words preceding the miscue. The reader should say, "Blank" for the miscued word, then continue onward through the text. This will help the reader to think about the context and to obtain the correct pronunciation of the word.
5. Place an acetate sheet over the reader's text. Have the reader read silently through the text, crossing out selected words in the text with a felt marker. The reader should then read the text aloud to the group or tutor, omitting the crossed-out words. The group or tutor must guess the omitted words by giving the exact word or a meaningful substitution. When the reader is finished, he or she should remove the sheet, wiping it off for reuse.
6. On laminated lined paper, the chalkboard, or an overhead transparency, place the miscued word in a new context. As the teacher, tutor, or parent writes, the reader should simultaneously read along. The reader may recognize the miscue in its new context. The reader should then be encouraged to recognize the miscue in the text.
7. After a text has been completely read, provide review for miscues or words with challenging meanings by:
   a. Placing the word or words in a new context using synonyms.

   Teacher/Tutor/Parent
   writes or says: The boy knew how to *mimic* the comedian, and

   Reader writes
   or says: his brother knew how to *imitate* the same comedian.

   b. Placing the word or words in a new context using antonyms.

   Teacher/Tutor/Parent
   writes or says: The man made an *insignificant* speech, but

   Reader writes
   or says: his opponent's speech was *important*.

8. Before the student reads the text, play a question/thinking game called *Agree or Disagree*. Using the vocabulary and the concepts from the text, ask questions. As you ask the questions the reader may skim and scan the book for answers. Such questions as the following might be asked:
   a. Do you agree or disagree that the Tyrannosaurus rex lived in the time of your grandmother?
   b. Do you agree or disagree that some dinosaurs were carnivores?

Comprehension

Inattention to Punctuation

1. Review the meanings of the various punctuation marks and discuss how they help with proper phrasing and the systematic organization of an author's thoughts. Provide numerous writing experiences so the reader begins to use punctuation marks as a means of making a message clear to another reader. Involvement in the writing process will help the reader to better understand the clues an author uses to convey meaning.

Insufficient Retellings and Improper Sequencing of Events

2. Ask the student to visualize and then verbally describe the events of a reading passage, including all pertinent details. Help the student to organize this description in the appropriate logic by asking such questions as, "What happened first, then second, third, etc.?"

3. Place a plastic sheet over a passage the student has read. Have the student underline and number the events as they occur in the passage with a felt marker. Have the student review the underlined and numbered portions and verbally describe the passage, including all properly sequenced facts.

4. Prior to the reading of the text, have the reader scout through the material, using all pictures, graphics, etc., to gather information. The reader should then be asked to predict the meaning by describing what he/she thinks will happen in this text.

5. Place an acetate sheet over the beginning portion of the text. Have the reader quickly scout through the material, finding and underlining words that help to reveal its meaning. Have the reader predict the meaning, describing what he/she thinks will happen in the text. (This could also be done orally by quickly scouting through the material and calling out relevant words or phrases.)

Types of Comprehension Question Weaknesses:
Main Idea, Terminology, Cause and Effect Relationships, Details

6. Ask the student or students to read a passage or story, and then write a short gist statement (main idea) on paper. The teacher, tutor, or parent should do the same. Then the statements should be read aloud. After hearing all statements, the most concise, yet thorough one should be discussed. An author may then choose to edit his/her statement. Edited statements may be kept in a folder and used for rereading and review.

7. Refer to recommendation #2, page 36.

8. Cause and effect (ce) Explain to the student that cause and effect questions involve a relationship of facts found in a text. Have the student read a passage looking for relationships that tell the cause or effect. The teacher, tutor, or parent should ask the reader questions like: "Why did Sue fall into the river?" (asking for the cause); "What happened after the boy found the 100-dollar bill?" (asking for the effect).

   Find a story that describes the cause of an event. Ask the student to write or tell the ending of the story, producing the effect. Then turn the tables, finding a story that describes the effect, and ask the student to write or tell the ending of the story, producing the cause.

9. As the student reads, ask him/her to draw a mind map, identifying the main idea as the center of the map and using radiating lines from the central idea to important details. Have the student discuss the map, offering him/her the chance to reread the text to edit the map or add more details.

10. After the student has read a particular portion of the text, have him/her draw cartoon frames to depict the details of the text. Discuss the drawing, offering editing opportunities to add or delete frames.

11. As the student reads, have him/her take notes on three-by-five cards or small bits of paper. Discuss the text, telling the student that he/she may reread and then add more notes. Have the student arrange the notes on top of his/her desk in the logical manner. Have the student read and discuss the notes.

12. Place students in a small group or in pairs. Tell one student to read aloud to the group. When finished, he/she must ask questions about the text. (Initially questions will be on the literal level. Teach students how to format questions to get different kinds of responses.) The first reader passes to another reader, and the same questioning procedure is followed.

Context Clues

13. Make a tape recording of a passage in which all difficult words are omitted. Give the student a copy of the passage and have him/her fill in the blanks as the tape is played. Accept meaningful substitutions.

14. Add homographs to the vocabulary file. Have the student or students write sentences or mini-stories using them in a context. Have students edit the sentences or stories and place them in a class-made book. Examples might look like the following:

    a. The man held a small lead pipe in his hand. "We will lead our team to victory!" she declared. (sentences)

    b. The bus driver knew that the driving would really be tough. The bus would have to wind around mountainous roads, and the heavy wind would cause the bus to sway back and forth. Despite all of this, he was determined to complete the journey. (mini-story)

FORM A

	(Primer)		(1)		(2)
1.	not	1.	kind	1.	mile
2.	funny	2.	rocket	2.	fair
3.	book	3.	behind	3.	ago
4.	thank	4.	our	4.	need
5.	good	5.	men	5.	fourth
6.	into	6.	met	6.	lazy
7.	know	7.	wish	7.	field
8.	your	8.	told	8.	taken
9.	come	9.	after	9.	everything
10.	help	10.	ready	10.	part
11.	man	11.	barn	11.	save
12.	now	12.	next	12.	hide
13.	show	13.	cat	13.	instead
14.	want	14.	hold	14.	bad
15.	did	15.	story	15.	love
16.	have	16.	turtle	16.	breakfast
17.	little	17.	give	17.	reach
18.	cake	18.	cry	18.	song
19.	home	19.	fight	19.	cupcake
20.	soon	20.	please	20.	trunk

(3)	(4)
1. beginning	1. worm
2. thankful	2. afford
3. written	3. player
4. reason	4. scientific
5. bent	5. meek
6. patient	6. rodeo
7. manage	7. festival
8. arithmetic	8. hillside
9. burst	9. coward
10. bush	10. boom
11. gingerbread	11. booth
12. tremble	12. freeze
13. planet	13. protest
14. struggle	14. nervous
15. museum	15. sparrow
16. grin	16. level
17. ill	17. underground
18. alarm	18. oxen
19. cool	19. eighty
20. engine	20. shouldn't

(5)

1. abandon
2. zigzag
3. terrific
4. terrify
5. plantation
6. loaf
7. hike
8. relative
9. available
10. grief
11. physical
12. commander
13. error
14. woodcutter
15. submarine
16. ignore
17. disappointed
18. wrestle
19. vehicle
20. international

(6)

1. seventeen
2. annoy
3. dwindle
4. rival
5. hesitation
6. navigator
7. gorge
8. burglar
9. construction
10. exploration
11. technical
12. spice
13. spike
14. prevail
15. memorial
16. initiation
17. undergrowth
18. ladle
19. walnut
20. tributary

Pat sat by the tree.

"Mom wants me to work," Pat said.

"I do not want to help her work.

I will hide by this big tree.

She will not find me.

I will hide from her.

My mom will not find me.

I will hide by this big tree!"

Terry got into the little car. He had something for Show and Tell in a big paper bag. Next, Bill got into the car with his big paper bag.

Then Ann got into the car. She had something for Show and Tell in a big paper bag, too. Last, Sue got into the car with her paper bag. Now the little car was ready to go to school.

"The little car is getting fat!" said Terry.

The children laughed.

Whiz! The baseball went right by me, and I struck at the air!

"Strike one," called the man. I could feel my legs begin to shake!

Whiz! The ball went by me again, and I began to feel bad. "Strike two," screamed the man.

I held the bat back because this time I would kill the ball! I would hit it right out of the park! I was so scared that I bit down on my lip. My knees shook and my hands grew wet.

Swish! The ball came right over the plate. Crack! I hit it a good one! Then I ran like the wind. Everyone was yelling for me because I was now a baseball star!

The sunlight shined into the mouth of the cave so Mark could see easily at first, but the farther he walked, the darker it grew. Boxer ran off to explore on his own.

Soon it grew so dark Mark could see nothing, but he could hear water dripping off the cave walls. He touched a wall with his hand to find it cold and damp. Mark began to grow fearful, so he lit his candle and held it high to look around.

Suddenly, the flame went out. He heard a low growl near him and saw a pair of fierce, green eyes glowing in the dark! He tried to relight the candle, but the first match went out! Finally, Mark's shaking hand held the lighted candle high.

"Boxer!" he shouted. "Now I recognize those green eyes of yours! Let's get out of here!"

The three were growing tired from their long journey, and now they had to cross a river. It was wide and deep, so they would have to swim across.

The younger dog plunged into the icy water barking for the others to follow him. The older dog jumped into the water. He was weak and suffering from pain, but somehow he managed to struggle to the opposite bank.

The poor cat was left all alone. He was so afraid that he ran up and down the bank wailing with fear. The younger dog swam back and forth trying to help. Finally, the cat jumped and began swimming near his friend.

At that moment something bad happened. An old beaver dam from upstream broke. The water came rushing downstream hurling a large log toward the animals. It struck the cat and swept him helplessly away.

"Look out," Sheila Young thought as she saw her challenger's bicycle come too close. "Watch out, you will foul me!"

At that moment a horrifying thing happened as she was bumped by another racer at forty miles an hour. Sheila's bicycle crashed, and she skidded to the surface of the track. From the wreck she received a nine-inch gash on her head.

The judges ruled that the race should be run again since a foul had been made. Sheila would not have enough time to get her wound stitched. Still, she didn't want to quit the race because she could think only of winning.

"Just staple the cut together with clamps," she told the doctor. "I want to try to win that race!"

The doctor did as Sheila asked. As she stood in silence while being treated, tears rolled down her face from the intense pain. Then, with a blood-stained bandage on her throbbing head, she pushed on to amaze the crowd with a victory and a gold medal!

"Thousands of people are dying on the battlefields from loss of blood," said Dr. Charles Drew. "I must give my time to solving the problems of blood transfusion."

Physicians had studied blood transfusion for years. However, they had met with many difficulties because the whole blood spoiled within days, and the matching of blood types was time-consuming. Nevertheless, Dr. Drew found there were fewer problems if plasma, instead of whole blood, was used in transfusion. Plasma, the liquid part of the blood without the cells, could be stored much longer and made the matching of blood types unnecessary. Anybody could be given plasma, and this was important on the battlefields of World War II.

In 1940 the Blood Transfusion Association set up a program for war-torn France. Dr. Drew asked them to send plasma rather than whole blood. But, it was started too late since France had fallen into the hands of the enemy.

Later, when Great Britain suffered heavy losses from air raids, Dr. Drew was asked to run a program called "Plasma for Britain." He organized the entire project, and thousands of Americans gave blood to help the British.

While he had been hiding out for the past five days, Johnny had given serious thought to the whole mess. He had decided to return home, turn himself in to the police, and take the consequences of his crime. Being only sixteen, he was too young to have to run away for the rest of his life. He knew the fight had been in self-defense, but the fact still remained that he had killed another person, and the thought of that miserable night in the city park sent Johnny into a terrifying panic.

He told Dally and Ponyboy of his decision, and now Dally reluctantly began the long drive home. Dally had gone to jail before, and this was one wretched experience he did not want his friend to have to endure.

As they reached the top of Jay Mountain, Dally slammed on the brakes! The old church where Johnny and Ponyboy had been hiding was in flames! Ponyboy and Johnny bolted from the car to question a bystander who explained that they were having a school picnic when the church began to burn.

Suddenly, the crowd was shocked to hear desperate cries from inside! Ponyboy and Johnny ran into the burning church, and the boys lifted the children one by one through a window to safety. Chunks of the old roof were already beginning to fall as the last child was taken out. Ponyboy leaped through the window, vaguely hearing the sound of falling timber. Then, as he lay coughing and exhausted on the ground, he heard Johnny's terrifying scream!

Witch-hunts were common in seventeenth-century England. The mere presence of a witch-hunter in a village caused such fear among the people that children would even denounce their parents.

Belief in magic was common in those days. Perhaps some of the victims of these hunts did think themselves guilty of witchery, but history has proven that the majority of men and women accused and tortured by witch-hunters were but poor, defenseless victims of the times.

One of the best-known methods for the detection of a witch was the "swimming test." In this ordeal the suspect was dragged into a pool or stream after he was already tired from torture and fear. If the suspect floated to the top he was found guilty, and long pins were plunged into his body in search of the devil's marks. If he sank to the bottom, he was presumed innocent.

In 1645 a man who titled himself Witchfinder General Matthew Hopkins led a severe and cruel hunt. Because a civil war was raging in England at the time, tensions and fears were common among the people. The time was ripe for persecution.

In that same year Hopkins imprisoned as many as 200 persons, all charged with witchcraft. Among eighteen of those who died by hanging was one John Lowes, a seventy-year-old clergyman who had been accused of witchcraft by his congregation. After undergoing intolerable torture, the old man admitted ownership of an evil spirit which he allegedly ordered to sink a ship. No one bothered to check out the existence of such a vessel or to ask about any reported sinkings on that day, and he was hanged after reading his own burial service.

"This lake is all treated sewer water," the old gentleman murmured in admiration. The old man sat on a bench as close to the bank as possible with his elbows resting on his knees while gazing at the rippling water. The breeze sweeping across the lake caused the sailboats to glide about with amazing ease.

"We are making great ecological strides," he thought to himself. He knew well the story of this remarkable lake nestled in the foothills of southern California. He swelled with pride to recall the wise choice the Santee citizens had made when they elected not to join the metropolitan sewage system where the waste would have been discharged into the Pacific with only inadequate primary treatment. Rather, the residents constructed their own sewage facility, reclaiming the sewer water, thus extending their own supply to provide basic needs and clean recreational extras.

"This is probably the only city park in the world which is built just yards downstream from a sewer plant," the gentleman thought. He leaned forward scooping up a handful of water. "This lake is more sanitary than most natural streams."

It had taken ingenious foresight to make this unprecedented plan viable. Its resourcefulness lay in the fact that clean water provided not only lucrative recreational facilities, but the sewage waste solids furnished marketable soil conditioners and plant fertilizers.

As the old gentleman arose he caught sight of paper trash carelessly tossed beside the shore. His contented expression changed to one of concern. He already knew that twenty million tons of paper are discarded each year in the United States representing a net loss of 340 million trees to the environment. The gentleman shook his head to think of this needless waste. He knew the United States comprises only 6 percent of the world's population, yet its citizens consume 30 percent of the world's total energy output, only to waste half of it. The old gentleman shuddered at these thoughts as he picked up the discarded paper and placed it into the trash container.

FORM A

Teacher Record

STUDENT RECORD SUMMARY SHEET

Student _____ Grade _____ Sex _____ Age _____
yrs. mos.

School _____ Administered by _____ Date _____

Grade	Word Lists	Graded Passages			Estimated Levels			
	% of words correct	WR Form____	Comp. Form____	Listen. Form____	Narrative			
Primer								Grade
1					Independent			_____
					Instructional			_____
2					Frustration			_____
					Listening			_____
3								
4	'				Expository			
5					Grade Level			
6					Science		Social Studies	
7					WR Comp.		WR Comp.	
8								
9								

Check consistent oral reading difficulties:

____ word-by-word reading
____ omissions
____ substitutions
____ corrections
____ repetitions
____ reversals
____ inattention to punctuation
____ word inserts
____ requests word help

Check consistent word recognition difficulties:

____ single consonants
____ consonant clusters
____ long vowels
____ short vowels
____ vowel digraphs
____ diphthongs
____ syllabication
____ use of context
____ basic sight
____ grade level sight

Check consistent comprehension difficulties:

____ main idea
____ factual
____ terminology
____ cause and effect
____ inferential
____ drawing conclusions
____ retelling

QUALITATIVE ANALYSIS SUMMARY SHEET

FORM_____

Level	# of Miscues	STUDENT: MISCUE IN CONTEXT	Meaning Change	DATE: NATURE OF MISCUE

If additional space is needed, permission is granted by the publisher to reproduce this summary sheet.

(Student Booklet page 42)

(Primer)	(1)	(2)
1. not_____	1. kind_____	1. mile_____
2. funny_____	2. rocket_____	2. fair_____
3. book_____	3. behind_____	3. ago_____
4. thank_____	4. our_____	4. need_____
5. good_____	5. men_____	5. fourth_____
6. into_____	6. met_____	6. lazy_____
7. know_____	7. wish_____	7. field_____
8. your_____	8. told_____	8. taken_____
9. come_____	9. after_____	9. everything_____
10. help_____	10. ready_____	10. part_____
11. man_____	11. barn_____	11. save_____
12. now_____	12. next_____	12. hide_____
13. show_____	13. cat_____	13. instead_____
14. want_____	14. hold_____	14. bad_____
15. did_____	15. story_____	15. love_____
16. have_____	16. turtle_____	16. breakfast_____
17. little_____	17. give_____	17. reach_____
18. cake_____	18. cry_____	18. song_____
19. home_____	19. fight_____	19. cupcake_____
20. soon_____	20. please_____	20. trunk_____

(3)

1. beginning_____
2. thankful_____
3. written_____
4. reason_____
5. bent_____
6. patient_____
7. manage_____
8. arithmetic_____
9. burst_____
10. bush_____
11. gingerbread_____
12. tremble_____
13. planet_____
14. struggle_____
15. museum_____
16. grin_____
17. ill_____
18. alarm_____
19. cool_____
20. engine_____

(4)

1. worm_____
2. afford_____
3. player_____
4. scientific_____
5. meek_____
6. rodeo_____
7. festival_____
8. hillside_____
9. coward_____
10. boom_____
11. booth_____
12. freeze_____
13. protest_____
14. nervous_____
15. sparrow_____
16. level_____
17. underground_____
18. oxen_____
19. eighty_____
20. shouldn't_____

(Student Booklet page 44)

(5)

1. abandon _____
2. zigzag _____
3. terrific _____
4. terrify _____
5. plantation _____
6. loaf _____
7. hike _____
8. relative _____
9. available _____
10. grief _____
11. physical _____
12. commander _____
13. error _____
14. woodcutter _____
15. submarine _____
16. ignore _____
17. disappointed _____
18. wrestle _____
19. vehicle _____
20. international _____

(6)

1. seventeen _____
2. annoy _____
3. dwindle _____
4. rival _____
5. hesitation _____
6. navigator _____
7. gorge _____
8. burglar _____
9. construction _____
10. exploration _____
11. technical _____
12. spice _____
13. spike _____
14. prevail _____
15. memorial _____
16. initiation _____
17. undergrowth _____
18. ladle _____
19. walnut _____
20. tributary _____

Primer (50 words   8 sent.)

**Examiner's Introduction
(Student Booklet page 45):**
Pat is thinking about fooling Mom. Have you ever thought about tricking your folks? Please read about Pat.

Pat sat by the tree.

"Mom wants me to work," Pat said.

"I do not want to help her work.

I will hide by this big tree.

She will not find me.

I will hide from her.

My mom will not find me.

I will hide by this big tree!"

**Comprehension Questions
and Possible Answers**

(mi) 1. What is this story about?
(Hiding from mom, getting out of work, etc.)

(f) 2. Where is Pat sitting?
(by the big tree)

(t) 3. What does the word *work* mean in this story?
(to do a chore or to do something you are supposed to do)

(ce) 4. Why is Pat going to hide by the big tree?
(so Pat's mom will not find Pat)

(f) 5. What does Pat's mom want Pat to do?
(help her work)

(inf) 6. What is said in the story which makes you think Pat doesn't want to work?
(Stated: I don't want to help her work, so I'll hide from her.)

Miscue Count:

O____ I____ S____ A____ REP____ REV____

Scoring Guide		
Word Rec.		Comp.
IND	0–1	IND 0
INST	2–3	INST 1–2
FRUST	5+	FRUST 3+

**Examiner's Introduction
(Student Booklet page 46):** In this story the young children are being picked up for school. Please read about this special day.

Terry got into the little car. He had something

for Show and Tell in a big paper bag. Next, Bill got

into the car with his big paper bag.

Then Ann got into the car. She had something

for Show and Tell in a big paper bag, too. Last, Sue

got into the car with her paper bag. Now the little

car was ready to go to school.

"The little car is getting fat!" said Terry.

The children laughed.

**Comprehension Questions
and Possible Answers**

(mi) 1. What is this story about?
(The day for Show and Tell, going to school for Show and Tell, etc.)

(f) 2. How did the children carry their things to school?
(in paper bags)

(ce) 3. What happened after the last child got into the car?
(The little car was ready to go to school.)

(f) 4. What did the children do when Terry said, "The little car is getting fat"?
(They laughed.)

(t) 5. In this story what does the word *ready* mean?
(all set to go to school or the car was full)

(inf) 6. What did Terry mean when he said that he thought the little car was getting fat?
(The car was getting crowded.)

Miscue Count:

O___I___S___A___REP___REV___

Scoring Guide	
Word Rec.	Comp.
IND 0–1	IND 0
INST 3–4	INST 1–2
FRUST 8+	FRUST 3+

Form A / Teacher Record / Graded Paragraphs

Level 2 (118 words   13 sent.)

Imagine how you would feel if you were up to bat and this was your team's last chance to win the game! Please read this story.

Whiz! The baseball went right by me, and I struck at the air!

"Strike one," called the man. I could feel my legs begin to shake!

Whiz! The ball went by me again, and I began to feel bad. "Strike two," screamed the man.

I held the bat back because this time I would kill the ball! I would hit it right out of the park! I was so scared that I bit down on my lip. My knees shook and my hands grew wet.

Swish! The ball came right over the plate. Crack! I hit it a good one! Then I ran like the wind. Everyone was yelling for me because I was now a baseball star!

Comprehension Questions
and Possible Answers

(mi) 1. What is this story about?
(a baseball game, someone who gets two strikes and finally gets a hit, etc.)

(f) 2. After the second strike, what did the batter plan to do?
(hit the ball right out of the park)

(inf) 3. Who was the "man" in this story who called the strikes?
(the umpire)

(t) 4. In this story, what was meant when the batter said, "I would kill the ball"?
(hit it very hard)

(ce) 5. Why was the last pitch a good one?
(because it went right over the plate)

(ce) 6. What did the batter do after the last pitch?
(The batter hit it a good one and ran like the wind.)

Miscue Count:

O_____I_____S_____A_____REP_____REV_____

Scoring Guide	
Word Rec.	Comp.
IND 1	IND 0
INST 6	INST 1–2
FRUST 12 +	FRUST 3 +

**Examiner's Introduction
(Student Booklet page 48):**

Mark's dad had warned him not to go near the cave, but Mark and his dog, Boxer, had ideas of their own. Please read this story.

The sunlight shined into the mouth of the cave so Mark could see easily at first, but the farther he walked, the darker it grew. Boxer ran off to explore on his own.

Soon it grew so dark Mark could see nothing, but he could hear water dripping off the cave walls. He touched a wall with his hand to find it cold and damp. Mark began to grow fearful, so he lit his candle and held it high to look around.

Suddenly, the flame went out. He heard a low growl near him and saw a pair of fierce, green eyes glowing in the dark! He tried to relight the candle, but the first match went out! Finally, Mark's shaking hand held the lighted candle high.

"Boxer!" he shouted. "Now I recognize those green eyes of yours! Let's get out of here!"

**Comprehension Questions
and Possible Answers**

(mi) 1. In this story what were Mark and Boxer doing?
(exploring a cave)

(f) 2. In what part of the cave was the sunlight?
(the mouth of the cave)

(f) 3. When they first entered the cave, what did Boxer do?
(ran off to explore on his own)

(t) 4. What is meant by the word *farther*?
(Mark went a greater distance into the cave.)

(t) 5. What is meant by the word *recognize*?
(to see something that you know)

(ce) 6. Why did Mark light the candle the first time?
(It grew dark and he got scared.)

(inf) 7. What makes you think Mark was scared when the candle went out?
(He tried to relight the candle and his hand shook.)

(f) 8. What were the low growl and the fierce, green eyes?
(his dog, Boxer)

Miscue Count:

O___I___S___A___REP___REV___

Scoring Guide	
Word Rec.	Comp.
IND 1–2	IND 0
INST 7–8	INST 2
FRUST 15+	FRUST 4+

**Examiner's Introduction
(Student Booklet page 49):**

If you like excitement then you will enjoy reading the *Incredible Journey* by Sheila Burnford. This story is about three pets, a cat and two dogs, whose owners leave the animals when they move to another country. The animals decide to try to find their owners but face many hardships. Please read a retelling of one of the incidents from this exciting story.

The three were growing tired from their long journey, and now they had to cross a river. It was wide and deep, so they would have to swim across.

The younger dog plunged into the icy water, barking for the others to follow him. The older dog jumped into the water. He was weak and suffering from pain, but somehow he managed to struggle to the opposite bank.

The poor cat was left all alone. He was so afraid that he ran up and down the bank wailing with fear. The younger dog swam back and forth trying to help. Finally, the cat jumped and began swimming near his friend.

At that moment something bad happened. An old beaver dam from upstream broke. The water came rushing downstream hurling a large log toward the animals. It struck the cat and swept him helplessly away.

**Comprehension Questions
and Possible Answers**

(mi) 1. In this passage what was the difficult thing the animals had to do?
(cross a river)

(f) 2. How would the animals get across the river?
(They would have to swim.)

(t) 3. What is the meaning of *plunged*?
(to jump in quickly)

(ce) 4. Why did the younger dog bark at the other animals?
(to try to get them to follow him)

(f) 5. What is meant by the phrase "wailing with fear"?
(to be so scared that one cries out)

(f) 6. After the cat jumped in, what bad thing happened?
(An old beaver dam broke.)

(ce) 7. Why did the log come hurling downstream?
(The rushing water brought it.)

(con) 8. What makes you think the animals were run down and in poor health?
(Stated: They were tired; the old dog was suffering from pain.)

Miscue Count:

Scoring Guide		
Word Rec.		Comp.
IND	1–2	IND	0–1
INST	7–8	INST	2
FRUST	15+	FRUST	4+

O____I____S____A____REP____REV____

Examiner's Introduction (Student Booklet page 50): Sheila Young enjoys bicycling and once competed in World and Olympic championship races. Please read about something that happened to Sheila during a cycling race. This passage is based upon information from an article entitled, "Sportswomanlike Conduct," appearing in a 1974 issue of *Newsweek*.

"Look out," Sheila Young thought as she saw her challenger's bicycle come too close. "Watch out, you will foul me!"

At that moment a horrifying thing happened as she was bumped by another racer at forty miles an hour. Sheila's bicycle crashed, and she skidded to the surface of the track. From the wreck she received a nine-inch gash on her head.

The judges ruled that the race should be run again since a foul had been made. Sheila would not have enough time to get her wound stitched. Still, she didn't want to quit the race because she could think only of winning.

"Just staple the cut together with clamps," she told the doctor. "I want to try to win that race!"

The doctor did as Sheila asked. As she stood in silence while being treated, tears rolled down her face from the intense pain. Then, with a blood-stained bandage on her throbbing head, she pushed on to amaze the crowd with a victory and a gold medal!

Comprehension Questions and Possible Answers

(mi)   1. In this passage, what horrifying thing happened to Sheila Young?
(She was fouled, causing a wreck and injury.)

(t)   2. What is a "challenger"?
(someone who says they can beat you in competition; another competitor)

(f)   3. What injury did Sheila receive in the wreck?
(a nine-inch gash on her head)

(ce)   4. In this passage, why didn't she want to quit the race?
(She could think only of winning.)

(f)   5. What did she ask the doctor to do for her?
(staple the cut with a clamp)

(t)   6. What is meant by the phrase "intense pain"?
(strong pain)

(ce)   7. Why did tears run down Sheila's face?
(As she was being treated, her wound was painful.)

(con) 8. What is said in the story that makes you think this race was an important one?
(Stated: Even though she had been hurt, the judges could not delay the race for her sake; the prize was a gold medal.)

Miscue Count:

O___ I___ S___ A___ REP___ REV___

Scoring Guide	
Word Rec.	Comp.
IND 2	IND 0–1
INST 9	INST 2
FRUST 18+	FRUST 4+

Level 6 (192 words   12 sent.)

**Examiner's Introduction
(Student Booklet page 51):**

Dr. Charles Drew overcame many obstacles to become a remarkable black American surgeon. Dr. Drew, who died in an auto crash at the age of forty-six, lived a life of dedication and kindness. The following information was derived from a book entitled, *Black Pioneers of Science and Invention*, by Louis Haber.

"Thousands of people are dying on the battlefields from loss of blood," said Dr. Charles Drew. "I must give my time to solving the problems of blood transfusion."

Physicians had studied blood transfusion for years. However, they had met with many difficulties because the whole blood spoiled within days, and the matching of blood types was time-consuming. Nevertheless, Dr. Drew found there were fewer problems if plasma, instead of whole blood, was used in transfusion. Plasma, the liquid part of the blood without the cells, could be stored much longer and made the matching of blood types unnecessary. Anybody could be given plasma, and this was important on the battlefields of World War II.

In 1940 the Blood Transfusion Association set up a program for war-torn France. Dr. Drew asked them to send plasma rather than whole blood. But it was started too late since France had fallen into the hands of the enemy.

Later, when Great Britain suffered heavy losses from air raids, Dr. Drew was asked to run a program called "Plasma for Britain." He organized the entire project, and thousands of Americans gave blood to help the British.

**Comprehension Questions
and Possible Answers**

(mi)   1. What was the area of Dr. Drew's major work?
       (blood transfusion)

(t)   2. What is meant by the word *difficulties*?
       (problems)

(ce)   3. Why did Dr. Drew decide to devote his time to solving the problems of blood transfusion?
       (Thousands were dying on the battlefields of World War II.)

(f)   4. What is plasma?
(the liquid portion of the blood without cells)

(ce) 5. Why is plasma so useful?
(it can be stored much longer than whole blood or it made the matching of blood types unnecessary)

(f)   6. What is meant by the phrase, "fallen into the hands of the enemy"?
(France had been defeated or taken over by the enemy.)

(ce) 7. Why did Americans give blood to help their British neighbors?
(Britain had suffered heavy losses from air raids.)

(con) 8. What is said in this story that makes you think more people survived injuries on the battle-field because of Dr. Drew's work in blood transfusion?
(Stated: Plasma could be stored longer; with plasma, blood typing was unnecessary; anybody could be given plasma.)

Miscue Count:

O____I____S____A____REP____REV____

Scoring Guide	
Word Rec.	Comp.
IND 2	IND 0–1
INST 10	INST 2
FRUST 20+	FRUST 4+

**Examiner's Introduction
(Student Booklet page 52):**

S. E. Hinton wrote a very sensitive book called *The Outsiders*, showing the loyalties teen-agers in gangs have toward one another. In this passage, Johnny is in serious trouble, and his friends, Ponyboy and Dally, prefer to stick by him until he can decide how best to solve his problem. Please read a retelling of one of the incidents from this memorable book.

While he had been hiding out for the past five days, Johnny had given serious thought to the whole mess. He had decided to return home, turn himself in to the police, and take the consequences of his crime. Being only sixteen, he was too young to have to run away for the rest of his life. He knew the fight had been in self-defense, but the fact still remained that he had killed another person, and the thought of that miserable night in the city park sent Johnny into a terrifying panic.

He told Dally and Ponyboy of his decision, and now Dally reluctantly began the long drive home. Dally had gone to jail before, and this was one wretched experience he did not want his friend to have to endure.

As they reached the top of Jay Mountain, Dally slammed on the brakes! The old church where Johnny and Ponyboy had been hiding was in flames! Ponyboy and Johnny bolted from the car to question a bystander who explained that they were having a school picnic when the church began to burn.

Suddenly, the crowd was shocked to hear desperate cries from inside! Ponyboy and Johnny ran into the burning church, and the boys lifted the children one by one through a window to safety. Chunks of the old roof were already beginning to fall as the last child was taken out. Ponyboy leaped through the window, vaguely hearing the sound of falling timber. Then, as he lay coughing and exhausted on the ground, he heard Johnny's terrifying scream!

**Comprehension Questions
and Possible Answers**

(mi)   1. What difficult conflict did Johnny have to solve?
(He had committed a crime, and he had to decide whether to turn himself in to the police or to run away.)

(t)   2. What is meant by the phrase, "take the consequences"?
(take the punishment for his crime)

(f)   3. Where did the crime take place?
(in the city park)

(ce) 4. Why were Dally and the boys returning home?
      (Johnny had decided to return home and turn himself in.)

(ce) 5. Why did Dally slam on the brakes?
      (He saw the burning church.)

(f)   6. How did the boys get the childern out of the burning church?
      (lifted them through the window)

(t)   7. What is meant by the word *vaguely*?
      (not clearly defined, unclear)

(con) 8. What is said in the story that makes you think Johnny thought he should turn himself in?
      (Stated: He said that he was too young to run and hide for the rest of his life; the fact still remained that he had killed another person, and this was apparently something he felt he couldn't live with.)

Miscue Count:

O___ I___ S___ A___ REP___ REV___

Scoring Guide		
Word Rec.		Comp.
IND	2–3	IND	0–1
INST	13	INST	2
FRUST	26+	FRUST	4+

Form A / Teacher Record / Graded Paragraphs

**Examiner's Introduction
(Student Booklet page 53):**

Witch-hunts took place in England back in the 1600s. The following information was derived from an article entitled, "East Anglican and Essex Witches," from *Man, Myth, and Magic: An Illustrated Encyclopedia of the Supernatural.*

Witch-hunts were common in seventeenth-century England. The mere presence of a witch-hunter in a village caused such fear among the people that children would even denounce their parents.

Belief in magic was common in those days. Perhaps some of the victims of these hunts did think themselves guilty of witchery, but history has proven that the majority of men and women accused and tortured by witch-hunters were but poor, defenseless victims of the times.

One of the best-known methods for the detection of a witch was the "swimming test." In this ordeal the suspect was dragged into a pool or stream after he was already tired from torture and fear. If the suspect floated to the top he was found guilty, and long pins were plunged into his body in search of the devil's marks. If he sank to the bottom, he was presumed innocent.

In 1645 a man who titled himself Witchfinder General Matthew Hopkins led a severe and cruel hunt. Because a civil war was raging in England at the time, tensions and fears were common among the people. The time was ripe for persecution.

In that same year Hopkins imprisoned as many as 200 persons, all charged with witchcraft. Among eighteen of those who died by hanging was one John Lowes, a seventy-year-old clergyman who had been accused of witchcraft by his congregation. After undergoing intolerable torture, the old man admitted ownership of an evil spirit which he allegedly ordered to sink a ship. No one bothered to check out the existence of such a vessel or to ask about any reported sinkings on that day, and he was hanged after reading his own burial service.

**Comprehension Questions
and Possible Answers**

(mi)   1. What commonly happened in seventeenth-century England?
(witch-hunts)

(f)   2. According to this passage, what has history proven about witch-hunts?
(Most of the men and women accused and tortured for being witches were but poor and defenseless people.)

(ce)   3. Why would children even denounce their parents as witches?
(The mere presence of a witch-finder caused such fear among the people and children.)

(t)   4. What is meant by the phrase, "method of detection"?
(way of finding something out)

(ce)   5. In seventeenth-century England, why was the time ripe for persecution?
(A civil war was raging, causing tension and fear.)

(t)   6. What is meant by the word *allegedly*?
(asserted to be true or exist but not proven)

(f)   7. What did John Lowes allegedly do?
(owned an evil spirit which sank a ship)

(inf)   8. What is said in the story that makes you think the swimming test was unjust?
(Stated: If the accused person sank, thus being proven innocent, he or she was probably dead from drowning.)

Miscue Count:

O____ I____ S____ A____ REP____ REV____

Scoring Guide	
Word Rec.	Comp.
IND 3	IND 0–1
INST 15	INST 2
FRUST 30+	FRUST 4+

Form A / Teacher Record / Graded Paragraphs

Examiner's Introduction
(Student Booklet page 54):

This selection, based upon information from two articles appearing in a 1973 issue of *Plain Truth*, entitled, "Who's That Polluting My World?" and "How One Town Solves Pollution and Saves Water," describes some interesting facts concerning pollution and its control.

"This lake is all treated sewer water," the old gentleman murmured in admiration. The old man sat on a bench as close to the bank as possible with his elbows resting on his knees while gazing at the rippling water. The breeze sweeping across the lake caused the sailboats to glide about with amazing ease.

"We are making great ecological strides," he thought to himself. He knew well the story of this remarkable lake nestled in the foothills of southern California. He swelled with pride to recall the wise choice the Santee citizens had made when they elected not to join the metropolitan sewage system where the waste would have been discharged into the Pacific with only inadequate primary treatment. Rather, the residents constructed their own sewage facility, reclaiming the sewer water, thus extending their own supply to provide basic needs and clean recreational extras.

"This is probably the only city park in the world which is built just yards downstream from a sewer plant," the gentleman thought. He leaned forward scooping up a handful of water. "This lake is more sanitary than most natural streams."

It had taken ingenious foresight to make this unprecedented plan viable. Its resourcefulness lay in the fact that clean water provided not only lucrative recreational facilities, but the sewage waste solids furnished marketable soil conditioners and plant fertilizers.

As the old gentleman arose he caught sight of paper trash carelessly tossed beside the shore. His contented expression changed to one of concern. He already knew that twenty million tons of paper are discarded each year in the United States representing a net loss of 340 million trees to the environment. The gentleman shook his head to think of this needless waste. He knew the United States comprises only 6 percent of the world's population, yet its citizens consume 30 percent of the world's total energy output, only to waste half of it. The old gentleman shuddered at these thoughts as he picked up the discarded paper and placed it into the trash container.

**Comprehension Questions
and Possible Answers**

(mi) 1. What is the main idea of this passage?
(We are making progress in pollution control, but still there is needless waste.)

(t) 2. What is meant by the phrase *inadequate primary treatment*?
(insufficient water treatment)

(f) 3. Where is this remarkable lake?
(in Santee in southern California)

(ce) 4. What happened when the Santee citizens constructed their own sewage facility?
(It provided basic needs and clean recreational extras.)

(t) 5. What is meant by the phrase *an unprecedented plan*?
(one not done before)

(f) 6. How much of the world's total energy does the United States use?
(30 percent)

(ce) 7. Why did the old gentleman's expression change when he got up from the bench?
(He caught sight of paper trash carelessly tossed beside the shore.)

(inf) 8. What is said in the story that makes you think that the plan to reclaim the sewage water was ingenious and well thought-out?
(Stated: The clean water provided not only lucrative recreational facilities, but the waste solids furnished marketable soil conditioners and plant fertilizers.)

Miscue Count:

O____ I____ S____ A____ REP____ REV____

Scoring Guide	
Word Rec.	Comp.
IND 3–4	IND 0–1
INST 18	INST 2
FRUST 36+	FRUST 4+

FORM B

	(Primer)		(1)		(2)
1.	birthday	1.	town	1.	yet
2.	went	2.	bear	2.	minute
3.	fish	3.	sound	3.	act
4.	like	4.	party	4.	bunny
5.	something	5.	there	5.	empty
6.	blue	6.	these	6.	inside
7.	that	7.	don't	7.	squirrel
8.	they	8.	brown	8.	thumb
9.	train	9.	shoe	9.	grandmother
10.	what	10.	light	10.	dragon
11.	mother	11.	hair	11.	elephant
12.	ride	12.	water	12.	I'd
13.	house	13.	own	13.	threw
14.	new	14.	race	14.	beautiful
15.	here	15.	why	15.	roof
16.	paint	16.	hear	16.	through
17.	work	17.	fly	17.	leave
18.	stop	18.	grass	18.	unhappy
19.	away	19.	morning	19.	garden
20.	around	20.	animal	20.	branch

(3)

1. broom
2. hammer
3. log
4. step
5. question
6. wrinkle
7. invisible
8. vegetable
9. engineer
10. allow
11. knee
12. excitement
13. storm
14. repair
15. sweep
16. swept
17. million
18. buzz
19. doorbell
20. you've

(4)

1. zebra
2. liberty
3. mend
4. dolphin
5. ability
6. compound
7. gentlemen
8. holly
9. swamp
10. swarm
11. chill
12. wreck
13. solid
14. alphabet
15. holiday
16. equal
17. dull
18. shiver
19. they're
20. nonsense

(5)

1. splendor
2. mason
3. radiant
4. cease
5. fisherman
6. brief
7. distress
8. fake
9. false
10. gust
11. proceed
12. triumph
13. scuffle
14. operation
15. military
16. hull
17. genius
18. contribution
19. reverse
20. indicate

(6)

1. counterclockwise
2. diesel
3. mathematical
4. representative
5. accomplishment
6. extraordinary
7. congratulation
8. daily
9. odor
10. resemble
11. acquire
12. combine
13. opportunity
14. transparent
15. transport
16. cheap
17. fifteenth
18. phase
19. violet
20. woolen

"I will grow tall," said Sally.
"I will grow tall like my mom.
I will grow tall fast.
My face will grow too.
I know my nose will grow.
What if my nose does not grow?
Then my nose will be a little baby nose!
I will look very funny!"

"Hurry," said Sue Brown. "Hide the balloons, and then all of us hide! Hurry, but don't make a sound or say a word! I see Dad coming up the walk now!"

When Father came into the house he didn't see his children. All was still and he could hear nothing.

Then Father did hear and see something. He heard his children laughing, singing, and calling "Surprise!" He saw fat blue and green balloons flying in the air!

Swish! My pet mouse ran straight under our neighbor's chair! Our neighbor didn't hear him because he is quiet, as a mouse should be. If she had seen him she would have yelled her head off.

Zoom! Now my clever gray mouse is bouncing off the jam jar on the breakfast table. He is sliding on the milk left around my glass! He is dancing on my cupcake!

He loves drinking lemonade. He eats lots of honey and blueberries. He is silly, different, and really quite funny. I'll always love my dear little mouse.

Say, have you seen my sweet gray friend? You better look now because he is right under your chair!

Joe sat down on the sidewalk in front of the trading post with his buckskin jacket thrown over his shoulder. He felt worried because it was difficult to know what to do.

"Grandfather told me never to sell these blue beads. He said they would bring me good fortune and good health. Grandfather is a wise and understanding man. He is proud to be an American Indian. He remembers when his grandfather gave him these same beads. He has often told me many interesting stories of how his grandfather rode horses and hunted buffalo on the plains."

Joe held the string of beads high into the air toward the sunlight. "These are perfectly beautiful beads," he said out loud. "I can't sell them because I too am proud of my great past. Yes, I will keep the beads!"

Joel's Pa was storming mad! Joel Goss had journeyed far with the schoolmaster to help him collect some money, and now they had returned not with money but with two colts! His father was furious.

The news had spread throughout the county that one of the colts was very small, and people had already begun to laugh. Joel had hoped to calm his father's anger by convincing him of Little Bub's strength, but Mr. Goss was still raging with anger! He pounded his fist on the table shouting several commands! The schoolmaster must find another place to live! The colts could not stay on the property!

Then he turned to Joel. It was time that Joel leave his house and find a job. In the morning they would visit Miller Chase and ask him to take Joel to work in the sawmill. Joel felt shocked and hurt! How could he leave his own home and Little Bub?

"I know that I was last in the race," announced Robyn Smith, "but I am determined to be the best woman jockey! I want to ride race horses!"

It was a rainy morning in 1969, and as Robyn stood outside talking to the trainer, Frank Wright, she was so dripping wet that water came running out of the top of her boots. Many people had doubts about Robyn's riding ability, but Wright was sure she could be a successful rider. He decided to give her a first big chance.

By December of that same year she had proven herself by placing fourth in a race. Robyn not only had skill as a jockey, but she also had a way with horses which made them run fast for her.

Soon she became accepted by others as an excellent rider. She went on to highlight her career with a surprising victory riding a horse named North Star. This horse was known for being wild on the track, but Robyn was able to handle him. Together they outran a horse named Onion. This was a special victory for Robyn because later, in another race, Onion defeated the famous horse, Secretariat!

The explosion was horrible that tragic day in Cleveland, Ohio, in 1916. Thirty-two men were trapped in a tunnel 250 feet below Lake Erie. No one could enter the smoke-filled tunnel to rescue the survivors.

"Someone get Garrett Morgan to help those men down there," shouted a man from the crowd. "Morgan and his breathing device are the only chance those men have!"

Garrett Morgan and his brother quickly came to the aid of the men trapped in the tunnel. Morgan had invented what he called a "Breathing Device," later to be known as the gas mask. Two years before, Morgan's invention had been tested by filling an enclosed tent with the foulest, thickest smoke possible. Placing the device over his head, a man entered this suffocating atmosphere, stayed twenty minutes, and emerged unharmed! Later, using a poisonous gas in a closed room, another test also provided the same successful results.

Although not all lived, every man was brought to the surface by the brothers. It was Morgan's concern for safer working conditions that saved lives that day and in the years to come.

Kate sat in her senior biology class, but she wasn't hearing a single word the teacher was saying since her mind was thoroughly preoccupied. She could only think about Dave and her date with him last Friday night.

The entire thing was so confusing and distracting that she kept glancing sideways to where he was sitting near the windows. He was by far the most handsome boy at Tylerton High. He was tall, strong, with shaggy hair, and brilliant blue eyes, but there was something very different about Dave Burdick which she found difficult to accept. She knew that he was independent, and at times he seemed actually defiant. She found this disturbing. He always neglected his appearance as if he didn't care what others thought. He was an excellent football player, probably the best in the entire school, but he quit the team. He was stubborn and belligerent, and he would argue with anyone over anything. He never hung around the other kids, so it seemed to her that he was a loner. He drove an old Ford pickup, which had chicken feathers and farm tools scattered all over the floor. Kate felt that he was more interested in raising chickens than in having friends. Yet, even knowing all of these things, there was something crazy going on in her mind. To her surprise she found Dave Burdick fascinating and quite to her liking.

You've probably said something like this yourself, "I was so exhausted I was a walking zombie!" On the island of Haiti in the Caribbean Sea, belief in zombies and the supernatural is common.

A *zombie* is characterized as a resurrected body brought back to half-life by magic. A zombie walks with a faltering gait, keeps downcast eyes, speaks garbled words, if it speaks at all, and generally displays abnormal behavior.

Some stories have actually been written describing zombies. For example, there is one depicting a girl who was allegedly discovered working in a small shop four years after her death. Even though this story was published, it has not been definitely verified.

A magistrate from Haiti once told a convincing tale about a man who went blind after seeing a troupe of zombies marching in the hills. It was his feeling that this was no laughing matter. Then he went on to tell his own eyewitness yarn of a body which arose from its grave as a half-alive figure and walked about the graveyard. Of course he continued to tell that this was an enormous hoax. The following day, he examined the grave to find a pipe leading from it to the fresh air where the imposter could breathe!

Supposedly, zombies can be owned by a living person. It is said if zombies are given something salty to eat or drink they will awaken from their trance. Thus, another tale has been told about a man whose wife mistakenly fed his zombies some salted biscuits. Awakened from their trance, these zombies hurried off to the cemetery, hurled themselves upon their graves, and attempted to dig themselves back into the earth.

As the Michaud family entered the village of Shimshal, the villagers abandoned their work and ran to welcome the travelers. They were the first Europeans the people of Shimshal had seen in twenty-seven years!

Shimshal, situated at an altitude of 10,000 feet, is the most remote village in Hunza. Located near a junction between China, the Soviet Union, Afghanistan, Pakistan and India, Hunza rests among the steep towers and deep gorges of the mountains.

The Michauds' journey took place in the spring of the year, so the danger of avalanches was always present. To reach Shimshal the party picked their way along the mountain ledges with painstaking care. Along the arduous trail lay several obstacles. For example, a suspension bridge consisting of stretched cables for handrails and planks for a footpath provided the only way to cross a dangerous river.

Shimshal has 5,000 to 6,000 inhabitants. Despite the fact that by Western standards these people are quite poor, the Michauds found them to be most generous and hospitable. They are a solid people living a life consisting of vigorous physical exercise, an adequate nutritional diet, and freedom from emotional stress. It is purported that many of them live to be as old as a century or more, thus attracting the attention of the outside world. Studies have been done to analyze the life-style of the Hunzakuts in an attempt to understand the secrets of longevity.

Their diet, consisting primarily of whole grains and fresh fruits, is of particular interest to the outside world. Because fuel is scarce, the food is minimally cooked and therefore maintains most of its nutritional value. Meat is rarely included in the diet because of limited pasture land. The Hunzakuts' steady nature is often attributed to dietary habits. At the turn of the century, a famous physician of British India wrote: "Their nerves are as solid as cables and sensitive as the strings of a violin."

FORM B

Teacher Record

STUDENT RECORD SUMMARY SHEET

Student _____ Grade _____ Sex _____ Age _____
yrs. mos.

School _____ Administered by _____ Date _____

Grade	Word Lists	Graded Passages			Estimated Levels			
	% of words correct	WR Form____	Comp. Form____	Listen. Form____	Narrative			
Primer								Grade
1					Independent			_____
2					Instructional			_____
					Frustration			_____
3					Listening			_____
4					Expository			
5					Grade Level			
6					Science		Social Studies	
7					WR Comp.		WR Comp.	
8								
9								

Check consistent oral reading difficulties:

____ word-by-word reading
____ omissions
____ substitutions
____ corrections
____ repetitions
____ reversals
____ inattention to punctuation
____ word inserts
____ requests word help

Check consistent word recognition difficulties:

____ single consonants
____ consonant clusters
____ long vowels
____ short vowels
____ vowel digraphs
____ diphthongs
____ syllabication
____ use of context
____ basic sight
____ grade level sight

Check consistent comprehension difficulties:

____ main idea
____ factual
____ terminology
____ cause and effect
____ inferential
____ drawing conclusions
____ retelling

QUALITATIVE ANALYSIS SUMMARY SHEET

FORM_____

Level	# of Miscues	STUDENT: MISCUE IN CONTEXT	Meaning Change	DATE: NATURE OF MISCUE

If additional space is needed, permission is granted by the publisher to reproduce this summary sheet.

(Student Booklet page 78)

(Primer)	(1)	(2)
1. birthday_____	1. town_____	1. yet_____
2. went_____	2. bear_____	2. minute_____
3. fish_____	3. sound_____	3. act_____
4. like_____	4. party_____	4. bunny_____
5. something_____	5. there_____	5. empty_____
6. blue_____	6. these_____	6. inside_____
7. that_____	7. don't_____	7. squirrel_____
8. they_____	8. brown_____	8. thumb_____
9. train_____	9. shoe_____	9. grandmother_____
10. what_____	10. light_____	10. dragon_____
11. mother_____	11. hair_____	11. elephant_____
12. ride_____	12. water_____	12. I'd_____
13. house_____	13. own_____	13. threw_____
14. new_____	14. race_____	14. beautiful_____
15. here_____	15. why_____	15. roof_____
16. paint_____	16. hear_____	16. through_____
17. work_____	17. fly_____	17. leave_____
18. stop_____	18. grass_____	18. unhappy_____
19. away_____	19. morning_____	19. garden_____
20. around_____	20. animal_____	20. branch_____

(Student Booklet page 79)

(3)

1. broom _____
2. hammer _____
3. log _____
4. step _____
5. question _____
6. wrinkle _____
7. invisible _____
8. vegetable _____
9. engineer _____
10. allow _____
11. knee _____
12. excitement _____
13. storm _____
14. repair _____
15. sweep _____
16. swept _____
17. million _____
18. buzz _____
19. doorbell _____
20. you've _____

(4)

1. zebra _____
2. liberty _____
3. mend _____
4. dolphin _____
5. ability _____
6. compound _____
7. gentlemen _____
8. holly _____
9. swamp _____
10. swarm _____
11. chill _____
12. wreck _____
13. solid _____
14. alphabet _____
15. holiday _____
16. equal _____
17. dull _____
18. shiver _____
19. they're _____
20. nonsense _____

(Student Booklet page 80)

(5)

1. splendor_____
2. mason_____
3. radiant_____
4. cease_____
5. fisherman_____
6. brief_____
7. distress_____
8. fake_____
9. false_____
10. gust_____
11. proceed_____
12. triumph_____
13. scuffle_____
14. operation_____
15. military_____
16. hull_____
17. genius_____
18. contribution_____
19. reverse_____
20. indicate_____

(6)

1. counterclockwise_____
2. diesel_____
3. mathematical_____
4. representative_____
5. accomplishment_____
6. extraordinary_____
7. congratulation_____
8. daily_____
9. odor_____
10. resemble_____
11. acquire_____
12. combine_____
13. opportunity_____
14. transparent_____
15. transport_____
16. cheap_____
17. fifteenth_____
18. phase_____
19. violet_____
20. woolen_____

Examiner's Introduction
(Student Booklet page 81): Sally is looking at herself in the mirror and has a silly thought about herself. Please read to see what she is thinking.

"I will grow tall," said Sally.

"I will grow tall like my mom.

I will grow tall fast.

My face will grow too.

I know my nose will grow.

What if my nose does not grow?

Then my nose will be a little baby nose!

I will look very funny!"

Comprehension Questions
and Possible Answers

(mi) 1. What is this story about?
(Sally grows tall, growing with a funny nose, etc.)

(f) 2. How does Sally think she will grow?
(tall, fast, like her mom)

(t) 3. In this story what does *funny* mean?
(odd, different, strange, possibly silly)

(t) 4. What does the word *grow* mean?
(to get bigger)

(ce) 5. What will happen if Sally's nose does not grow?
(She will have a baby nose.)

(inf) 6. Do you think Sally really believes that her nose will stay a baby nose?
(No, she says that she knows her nose will grow.)

Miscue Count:

O_____ I_____ S_____ A_____ REP_____ REV_____

Scoring Guide	
Word Rec.	Comp.
IND 0–1	IND 0
INST 2–3	INST 1–2
FRUST 5+	FRUST 3+

**Examiner's Introduction
(Student Booklet page 82):**

We all like special parties. You will now read about one given for someone very special.

"Hurry," said Sue Brown. "Hide the balloons, and then all of us hide! Hurry, but don't make a sound or say a word! I see Dad coming up the walk now!"

When Father came into the house he didn't see his children. All was still and he could hear nothing.

Then Father did hear and see something. He heard his children laughing, singing, and calling "Surprise!" He saw fat blue and green balloons flying in the air!

**Comprehension Questions
and Possible Answers**

(mi) 1. What is this story about?
(A surprise for Dad, a party for Dad, etc.)

(ce) 2. Why did Sue hurry to hide the balloons?
(Because Father was coming up the walk.)

(t) 3. In this story what is meant by the word walk?
(a concrete sidewalk)

(f) 4. What color balloons were flying in the air?
(blue and green)

(ce) 5. What did the children do after Father was in the house?
(The children laughed, sang, and called "Surprise!")

(con) 6. What is said in the story that makes you think the children were going to surprise their father?
(Stated: All was still; he couldn't see or hear anything.)

Miscue Count:

O____ I____ S____ A____ REP____ REV____

Scoring Guide	
Word Rec.	Comp.
IND 0–1	IND 0
INST 3–4	INST 1–2
FRUST 8+	FRUST 3+

**Examiner's Introduction
(Student Booklet page 83):**   You are about to read of a very special and rather extraordinary animal.

Swish! My pet mouse ran straight under our neighbor's chair! Our neighbor didn't hear him because he is quiet, as a mouse should be. If she had seen him she would have yelled her head off.

Zoom! Now my clever gray mouse is bouncing off the jam jar on the breakfast table. He is sliding on the milk left around my glass! He is dancing on my cupcake!

He loves drinking lemonade. He eats lots of honey and blueberries. He is silly, different, and really quite funny. I'll always love my dear little mouse.

Say, have you seen my sweet gray friend? You better look now because he is right under your chair!

**Comprehension Questions
and Possible Answers**

(mi) 1. What is a good title for this story?
("My Pet Mouse")

(f) 2. What color is this mouse?
(gray)

(t) 3. In this story, what is meant by *clever*?
(skillful, quick, smart)

(f) 4. What does this unusual mouse like to drink?
(lemonade)

(ce) 5. Why didn't the neighbor see or hear the mouse?
(The mouse is quiet, as a mouse should be.)

(con) 6. What is said in the story that makes you think that people might be scared of a mouse?
(Stated: The neighbor would have yelled her head off; you'd better look out because the mouse is under your chair!)

Miscue Count:

O____ I____ S____ A____ REP____ REV____

Scoring Guide	
Word Rec.	Comp.
IND 1	IND 0
INST 6	INST 1–2
FRUST 12 +	FRUST 3 +

Level 3 (138 words   12 sent.)

**Examiner's Introduction
(Student Booklet page 84):**

Joe wanted more than anything in the world to buy the electric train set in the trading post window. But should he do this? Please read the following story.

Joe sat down on the sidewalk in front of the trading post with his buckskin jacket thrown over his shoulder. He felt worried because it was difficult to know what to do.

"Grandfather told me never to sell these blue beads. He said they would bring me good fortune and good health. Grandfather is a wise and understanding man. He is proud to be an American Indian. He remembers when his grandfather gave him these same beads. He has often told me many interesting stories of how his grandfather rode horses and hunted buffalo on the plains."

Joe held the string of beads high into the air toward the sunlight. "These are perfectly beautiful beads," he said out loud. "I can't sell them because I too am proud of my great past. Yes, I will keep the beads!"

**Comprehension Questions
and Possible Answers**

(mi) 1. What is Joe's difficult decision?
       (whether to sell the beads his grandfather had given him)

(f)   2. Where was Joe sitting?
       (on the sidewalk in front of the trading post)

(f)   3. What did Joe's grandfather say the beads would do for Joe?
       (bring him good fortune and good health)

(t)   4. What is meant by the word *remembers*?
       (to recall from the past)

(f)   5. Who had given the beads to Joe's grandfather?
       (Joe's great-great grandfather or Joe's grandfather's grandfather)

(t)   6. In the phrase "hunted buffalo on the plains", what is meant by "on the plains"?
       (western great plains or large, flat country land)

(ce) 7. Why did Joe finally decide he couldn't sell the beads?
       (He was proud of his past.)

(con) 8. What is said in the story that makes you think Joe has respect for his grandfather?
       (Stated: Grandfather is a wise and understanding man; he couldn't sell the beads.)

Miscue Count:

O____ I____ S____ A____ REP____ REV____

Scoring Guide	
Word Rec.	Comp.
IND 1–2	IND 0–1
INST 7	INST 2
FRUST 14+	FRUST 4+

100

Form B / Teacher Record / Graded Paragraphs

Level 4 (157 words   13 sent.)

**Examiner's Introduction
(Student Booklet page 85):**

Justin Morgan Had A Horse, written by Marguerite Henry, is the thrilling story, set in colonial days, of a small runt work colt who grew to be the father of the famous American Morgan horses. Please read a retelling of one of the incidents from this exciting story.

Joel's Pa was storming mad! Joel Goss had journeyed far with the schoolmaster to help him collect some money, and now they had returned not with money but with two colts! His father was furious.

The news had spread throughout the county that one of the colts was very small, and people had already begun to laugh. Joel had hoped to calm his father's anger by convincing him of Little Bub's strength, but Mr. Goss was still raging with anger! He pounded his fist on the table shouting several commands! The schoolmaster must find another place to live! The colts could not stay on the property!

Then he turned to Joel. It was time that Joel leave his house and find a job. In the morning they would visit Miller Chase and ask him to take Joel to work in the sawmill. Joel felt shocked and hurt!

How could he leave his own home and Little Bub?

Comprehension Questions and Possible Answers

(mi) 1. In this story, why was Joel's father so angry?
(Joel and the schoolmaster had not returned from their journey with money, but rather with two unwanted colts.)

(t) 2. What is meant by the word *furious*?
(very mad or angry)

(ce) 3. Why had people begun to laugh about one of the colts?
(One of the colts was very small.)

(t) 4. What is meant by the word *commands* in the phrase "shouting several commands"?
(to give orders or to direct someone)

(f) 5. How had Joel hoped to calm his father's anger?
(by convincing him of Little Bub's strength)

(f) 6. What did Mr. Goss tell the schoolmaster he must do?
(find another place to live)

(f) 7. What did Mr. Goss tell Joel he must do?
(leave his house and find a job)

(inf) 8. What makes you think Joel was upset by what his father said to him?
(Stated: He felt shocked and hurt.)

Miscue Count:

O____ I____ S____ A____ REP____ REV____

Scoring Guide		
Word Rec.	Comp.	
IND 1–2	IND 0–1	
INST 7–8	INST 2	
FRUST 15+	FRUST 4+	

**Examiner's Introduction
(Student Booklet page 86):**

This is a story about Robyn Smith who left a career as a movie star to become one of the first female jockeys. The following information was derived from an article appearing in *The Lincoln Library of Sports Champions.*

"I know that I was last in the race," announced Robyn Smith, "but I am determined to be the best woman jockey! I want to ride race horses!"

It was a rainy morning in 1969, and as Robyn stood outside talking to the trainer, Frank Wright, she was so dripping wet that water came running out of the top of her boots. Many people had doubts about Robyn's riding ability, but Wright was sure she could be a successful rider. He decided to give her a first big chance.

By December of that same year she had proven herself by placing fourth in a race. Robyn not only had skill as a jockey, but she also had a way with horses which made them run fast for her.

Soon she became accepted by others as an excellent rider. She went on to highlight her career with a surprising victory riding a horse named North Star. This horse was known for being wild on the track, but Robyn was able to handle him. Together they outran a horse named Onion. This was a special victory for Robyn because later, in another race, Onion defeated the famous horse, Secretariat!

**Comprehension Questions
and Possible Answers**

(mi)   1. What was Robyn Smith determined to be?
    (the best woman jockey)

(ce)   2. Why did water run out of the top of Robyn's boots?
    (because she was standing outside in the rain)

(f)   3. What did Frank Wright do for Robyn?
    (gave her a first big chance)

(t)   4. What is meant by the phrase, "proven herself"?
    (She showed that she could ride well.)

(f)   5. What did others think of Robyn when she proved her riding skill?
    (She was accepted as a good jockey.)

6. What was the horse she rode known for?
(being wild on the track)

7. Why was this a special victory for Robyn?
(North Star defeated Onion; Onion defeated the famous horse Secretariat.)

8. Why do you think Robyn's trainer had confidence in her riding?
(Stated: Wright was sure she could be a successful rider; she had a way with horses which made them run fast for her; she had skill as a rider.)

Miscue Count:

O____ I____ S____ A____ REP____ REV____

Scoring Guide	
Word Rec.	Comp.
IND 2	IND 0–1
INST 9	INST 2
FRUST 18+	FRUST 4+

**Examiner's Introduction
(Student Booklet page 87):**

Garrett A. Morgan, a black American inventor, was born in 1877. He not only invented the first electric traffic signal but also other important inventions. The following information was derived from a book entitled, *Black Pioneers of Science and Invention*, by Louis Haber.

The explosion was horrible that tragic day in Cleveland, Ohio, in 1916. Thirty-two men were trapped in a tunnel 250 feet below Lake Erie. No one could enter the smoke-filled tunnel to rescue the survivors.

"Someone get Garrett Morgan to help those men down there," shouted a man from the crowd. "Morgan and his breathing device are the only chance those men have!"

Garrett Morgan and his brother quickly came to the aid of the men trapped in the tunnel. Morgan had invented what he called a "Breathing Device," later to be known as the *gas mask*. Two years before, Morgan's invention had been tested by filling an enclosed tent with the foulest, thickest smoke possible. Placing the device over his head, a man entered this suffocating atmosphere, stayed twenty minutes, and emerged unharmed! Later, using a poisonous gas in a closed room, another test also provided the same successful results.

Although not all lived, every man was brought to the surface by the brothers. It was Morgan's concern for safer working conditions that saved lives that day and in the years to come.

**Comprehension Questions
and Possible Answers**

(mi) 1. What did Garrett Morgan invent?
(gas mask—breathing device)

(f) 2. Where was the tunnel located in which the men were trapped?
(250 feet below Lake Erie)

(ce) 3. What happened as a result of the terrible explosion in Cleveland?
(thirty-two men were trapped)

(t) 4. What is meant by the phrase, "this suffocating atmosphere"?
(the air in the tent was without oxygen)

(t) 5. What is meant by the word *device*?
(something intricate in design; a machine)

(ce) 6. What happened to the man who stayed in the tent for twenty minutes?
(He emerged unharmed.)

(f)   7. What was used to test the gas mask the second time?
(a poisonous gas)

(inf)   8. What is said in the story that makes you think Morgan cared for the safety of others?
(Stated: It was Morgan's concern for safer working conditions which saved lives that day.)

Miscue Count:

O____ I____ S____ A____ REP____ REV____

Scoring Guide		
Word Rec.		Comp.
IND	2	IND	0–1
INST	10	INST	2
FRUST	20+	FRUST	4+

Level 7 (234 words   15 sent.)

**Examiner's Introduction
(Student Booklet page 88):**

Dave's Song, a book by Robert McKay, is a sensitive story about a girl who finds out that she can care for someone quite different from her other friends. Please read a retelling of part of this book.

Kate sat in her senior biology class, but she wasn't hearing a single word the teacher was saying since her mind was thoroughly preoccupied. She could only think about Dave and her date with him last Friday night.

The entire thing was so confusing and distracting that she kept glancing sideways to where he was sitting near the windows. He was by far the most handsome boy at Tylerton High. He was tall, strong, with shaggy hair, and brilliant blue eyes, but there was something very different about Dave Burdick which she found difficult to accept. She knew that he was independent, and at times he seemed actually defiant. She found this disturbing. He always neglected his appearance as if he didn't care what others thought. He was an excellent football player, probably the best in the entire school, but he quit the team. He was stubborn and belligerent, and he would argue with anyone over anything. He never hung around the other kids, so it seemed to her that he was a loner. He drove an old Ford pickup, which had chicken feathers and farm tools scattered all over the floor. Kate felt that he was more interested in raising chickens than in having friends. Yet, even knowing all of these things, there was something crazy going on in her mind. To her surprise she found Dave Burdick fascinating and quite to her liking.

**Comprehension Questions
and Possible Answers**

(mi) 1. Why was Kate confused and distracted?
(Dave was very different from her other friends, but she still found that she liked him.)

(ce) 2. Why didn't Kate hear anything the biology teacher was saying?
(She was preoccupied.)

(t) 3. What is meant by the word *independent*?
(not dependent upon others)

(f) 4. What did Kate find disturbing about Dave?
(his defiant attitude)

(t) 5. What is meant by the word *belligerent*?
(hostile, waging war)

(f) 6. What did Dave's truck have in it?
(chicken feathers and old farm tools)

106   Form B / Teacher Record / Graded Paragraphs

(ce) 7. Why did Kate think Dave was a loner?
(because he never hung around other kids)

(inf) 8. What is said in the story that makes you think Dave had a negative attitude?
(Stated: He seemed defiant, stubborn, belligerent.)

Miscue Count:

O___ I___ S___ A___ REP___ REV___

Scoring Guide	
Word Rec.	Comp.
IND 2–3	IND 0–1
INST 13	INST 2
FRUST 26+	FRUST 4+

Examiner's Introduction (Student Booklet page 89): The next selection is about zombies. Some people believe in them and some say there is a logical explanation for would-be zombies. The following information was derived from an article entitled, "Zombies," from *Man, Myth, and Magic: An Illustrated Encyclopedia of the Supernatural.*

You've probably said something like this yourself, "I was so exhausted I was a walking zombie!" On the island of Haiti in the Caribbean Sea, belief in zombies and the supernatural is common.

A *zombie* is characterized as a resurrected body brought back to half-life by magic. A zombie walks with a faltering gait, keeps downcast eyes, speaks garbled words, if it speaks at all, and generally displays abnormal behavior.

Some stories have actually been written describing zombies. For example, there is one depicting a girl who was allegedly discovered working in a small shop four years after her death. Even though this story was published, it has not been definitely verified.

A magistrate from Haiti once told a convincing tale about a man who went blind after seeing a troupe of zombies marching in the hills. It was his feeling that this was no laughing matter. Then he went on to tell his own eyewitness yarn of a body which arose from its grave as a half-alive figure and walked about the graveyard. Of course he continued to tell that this was an enormous hoax. The following day, he examined the grave to find a pipe leading from it to the fresh air where the imposter could breathe!

Supposedly, zombies can be owned by a living person. It is said if zombies are given something salty to eat or drink they will awaken from their trance. Thus, another tale has been told about a man whose wife mistakenly fed his zombies some salted biscuits. Awakened from their trance, these zombies hurried off to the cemetery, hurled themselves upon their graves, and attempted to dig themselves back into the earth.

Comprehension Questions and Possible Answers

(mi)   1. What is an unusual belief which exists in Haiti?
(belief in zombies, or the supernatural)

(t)   2. How does this passage define a *zombie*?
(a resurrected body brought back to half-life)

(f)   3. Where is Haiti located?
(in the Caribbean Sea)

(f)   4. How long after her alleged death had the girl been found working in the small shop?
(four years)

(t)   5. What is meant by the word *hoax*?
(a trick causing deception)

(ce) 6. Why was the imposter able to breathe?
(He had a pipe under the grave leading to the fresh air.)

(ce) 7. What happened when the man's wife fed the zombies salty biscuits?
(They awakened from their trance, hurried off to the cemetery and tried to bury themselves in their graves.)

(inf) 8. What is said that makes you think the magistrate took the tale about the zombies in the hills seriously?
(Stated: He said that it was no laughing matter.)

Miscue Count:

O____ I____ S____ A____ REP____ REV____

Scoring Guide	
Word Rec.	Comp.
IND 3	IND 0–1
INST 15	INST 2
FRUST 30+	FRUST 4+

Examiner's Introduction
(Student Booklet page 90):

In this story, a European family visits an isolated area in Asia called Hunza to study ancient traditions. They learned, however, that to find real traditions they must hike the dangerous mountain trails to Shimshal in Upper Hunza. This selection is based upon information taken from an article which appeared in *National Geographic*.

As the Michaud family entered the village of Shimshal, the villagers abandoned their work and ran to welcome the travelers. They were the first Europeans the people of Shimshal had seen in twenty-seven years!

Shimshal, situated at an altitude of 10,000 feet, is the most remote village in Hunza. Located near a junction between China, the Soviet Union, Afghanistan, Pakistan and India, Hunza rests among the steep towers and deep gorges of the mountains.

The Michauds' journey took place in the spring of the year, so the danger of avalanches was always present. To reach Shimshal the party picked their way along the mountain ledges with painstaking care. Along the arduous trail lay several obstacles. For example, a suspension bridge consisting of stretched cables for handrails and planks for a footpath provided the only way to cross a dangerous river.

Shimshal has 5,000 to 6,000 inhabitants. Despite the fact that by Western standards these people are quite poor, the Michauds found them to be most generous and hospitable. They are a solid people living a life consisting of vigorous physical exercise, an adequate nutritional diet, and freedom from emotional stress. It is purported that many of them live to be as old as a century or more, thus attracting the attention of the outside world. Studies have been done to analyze the life-style of the Hunzakuts in an attempt to understand the secrets of longevity.

Their diet, consisting primarily of whole grains and fresh fruits, is of particular interest to the outside world. Because fuel is scarce, the food is minimally cooked and therefore maintains most of its nutritional value. Meat is rarely included in the diet because of limited pasture land. The Hunzakuts' steady nature is often attributed to dietary habits. At the turn of the century, a famous physician of British India wrote:

"Their nerves are as solid as cables and sensitive as the strings of a violin."

Comprehension Questions and Possible Answers

(mi) 1. What is the main idea of this article?
(The Michaud family visited a remote village in Hunza, bringing knowledge of this land's traditions to the Western world.)

(f) 2. Where is Shimshal located?
(at an altitude of 10,000 feet in the land of Hunza)

(t) 3. What is meant by the word *arduous*?
(hard to accomplish or achieve)

(f) 4. Despite the fact that the people are poor, what is their disposition like?
(generous and hospitable)

(t) 5. What is meant by the phrase, *"freedom from emotional stress"*?
(their society is free from mental tension)

(ce) 6. Why have studies been done on the life-style of the Hunzakuts?
(in an attempt to understand the secrets of longevity)

(ce) 7. Why is their food minimally cooked?
(fuel is so scarce)

(con) 8. What is said in the story that makes you think the Hunzakuts are good-natured people?
(Stated: They are generous and hospitable; they are a solid yet sensitive people; they have a steady nature.)

Miscue Count:

O____ I____ S____ A____ REP____ REV____

Scoring Guide		
Word Rec.		Comp.
IND	3–4	IND	0–1
INST	18	INST	2
FRUST	36+	FRUST	4+

FORM C

_____

Student Booklet

(Primer)	(1)	(2)
1. about	1. ice	1. goose
2. can	2. before	2. mouse
3. who	3. another	3. library
4. with	4. children	4. teacher
5. some	5. stopped	5. kite
6. goat	6. hurry	6. cart
7. out	7. drop	7. different
8. trees	8. friend	8. anyone
9. father	9. balloon	9. feather
10. red	10. when	10. pie
11. green	11. where	11. sidewalk
12. make	12. those	12. straight
13. is	13. picnic	13. telephone
14. yes	14. laugh	14. clean
15. saw	15. farm	15. remember
16. get	16. airplane	16. wood
17. ball	17. tomorrow	17. summer
18. and	18. wagon	18. bell
19. down	19. made	19. gun
20. are	20. surprise	20. matter

(3)

1. clap
2. fright
3. diamond
4. silence
5. nurse
6. wiggle
7. precious
8. salt
9. bread
10. breath
11. fellow
12. several
13. unusual
14. overhead
15. driven
16. fool
17. darkness
18. honor
19. screen
20. they'll

(4)

1. canoe
2. hasn't
3. dozen
4. motion
5. pride
6. vicious
7. concern
8. harvest
9. sample
10. official
11. windshield
12. human
13. humor
14. decorate
15. slender
16. seventh
17. parachute
18. good-bye
19. dignity
20. trudge

(5)

1. prevent
2. kindle
3. grease
4. typical
5. foam
6. blur
7. mumps
8. telegram
9. vision
10. sandal
11. argument
12. hail
13. halt
14. region
15. manager
16. sleet
17. yarn
18. parallel
19. coconut
20. dissolve

(6)

1. midstream
2. lens
3. bail
4. college
5. failure
6. falter
7. width
8. graceful
9. somewhat
10. privacy
11. microphone
12. particle
13. clutter
14. applaud
15. vapor
16. reluctant
17. contract
18. nephew
19. insurance
20. fund

Look! It is me!
I can run as fast as a train!
I can jump over a big tall tree!
I can ride my bike as fast as a running goat!
I can see very little things far away.
I can put on a good show!
Yes, I am something!

I found a lost baby turtle. I took him home so he could live in my house. A friend gave me his prize rabbit. I took the rabbit home to live in my house.

I found a lost duck so I took her home too. I saw a little, cold blackbird and took him home. Then, I saw a cow who looked so sad. I took her home!

But Mom said, "No! No! Not a cow!"

"Look out, you'll get hit!" I yelled as Shep ran across the busy road. "Thud!" was the noise I heard, and then I saw my pup lying in the street. "Oh, no!" I shouted. I felt scared inside.

"Shep is my best friend!" I wanted to cry out. I knew that he was hurt, but he'd be all right if I could get help fast. I knew I had to be brave.

"Mom! Dad!" I yelled as I ran straight home. I tried to fight back the tears. But they started rolling down my face anyway as I blasted through the door. "Shep has been hit, and he's badly hurt!" I cried out. "Please hurry and help him!"

FOR NEIGHBORHOOD TIGERS ONLY! KNOCK ONE THOUSAND TIMES AND SAY THE SECRET WORD BEFORE ENTERING!

These were the signs which Jack read as he stood outside the neighborhood clubhouse. Jack was a new boy, and he really wanted to belong to the club. "How can I get the kids to agree to let me belong?" he thought. Suddenly he dashed home and soon returned with a bucket of yellow paint, one of black, and several brushes. He began pounding on the clubhouse door.

"I'm knocking a thousand times!" he shouted. "I don't know the secret word," he declared, "but I have something important to tell everyone! I'm the new boy," he explained. "Since the name of your club is 'Tigers,' I thought you might want to paint your clubhouse yellow with black stripes!"

All the kids thought this was a great idea and quickly invited Jack to belong!

Jody was so worried that he didn't even care to eat. He had stayed in the barn all day to take care of his sick pony, Gabilan. The pony's condition was growing worse as his breathing grew louder and harder.

At nightfall Jody brought a blanket from the house so he could sleep near Gabilan. In the middle of the night a wind whipped around the barn and blew the door open.

At dawn Jody awakened to the banging of the barn door. Gabilan was gone! In alarm he ran from the barn following the pony's tracks. Looking upward he saw buzzards, the birds of death, flying overhead. Jody stood still, then ran to the top of a small hill. In a clearing below, he saw something that filled his heart with anger and hate. A buzzard was perched on his dying pony's head.

"I want to be the fastest woman driver in the world," stated Shirley Muldowney. "I'd really like to go 500 miles per hour, but I'll be happy to go 400 this year and try for 500 next year," she quickly added.

Shirley, nicknamed Cha Cha, is presently the only woman licensed to drive Top Fuel cars. These cars are the fastest, the most powerful, and among the most carefully built machines in the car racing sport. Not only is she licensed to drive Top Fuel cars, but she is now one of the top challengers in the country. She has established a top speed of 241.58 miles per hour. No Top Fuel driver has reached a speed of over 250 miles per hour.

Shirley has a great deal of energy, determination, and nerve. She is confident that she can drive her car to victory. It is characteristic of her to accomplish about anything she sets out to do. A good friend has said, "It's been a long time since people thought of her just as a woman who drives race cars. She's a top driver who just happens to be a woman!"

James Cornish lay wounded on the saloon floor! "He's been stabbed in the chest!" shouted one horrified bystander. "Someone get him to a hospital!" another shouted.

It was a hot and humid day in Chicago in 1893. Cornish arrived at the hospital with a one-inch knife wound in his chest, dangerously near his heart. Dr. Daniel Hale Williams was called in to operate.

In those days when blood transfusions and antibiotics were unknown, chest surgery was rarely attempted since it meant a high risk of death. As Dr. Williams began to operate, he found that the stab wound had cut the heart and the sac around the heart. Dr. Williams then made history by becoming the first surgeon to successfully operate on the human heart.

Dr. Williams did not release this information for three and a half years. When he did, the newspaper headline read, "Sewed Up His Heart," and the news became known to the entire world. Not only had Cornish been discharged from the hospital a well man, but he lived fifty years after his surgery. Cornish even outlived the surgeon who had saved his life.

Jim was sixteen years old, and he thought more of his older brother, Kevin, than anyone else. He had informed all his friends that he'd not see them during the summer because he would be spending all his time with Kevin. It would be a terrific summer because Kevin was the greatest guy in the world.

But when Kevin arrived home from his first year at college something was different about him; he seemed unsettled, stayed confined to his room, and requested that Jim not disturb him. He wasn't interested in talking over old times. In fact, everything seemed to bore him.

Soon Jim discovered that Kevin had changed. Kevin smoked grass and spent his days beating the streets looking for LSD. Jim was stunned, bewildered, and to make things worse, it seemed to him that their parents didn't notice any unusual change in Kevin's personality.

Then one evening that inevitable occurrence which goes along with the drug scene happened. Kevin had taken the LSD near the time their folks left the house. It wasn't long before Jim found his brother convulsing, writhing on the floor, hallucinating, and unconsciously screaming out crazy things.

It was a frightful experience for Jim to see Kevin in such torture. He was terrorized with fear as he hurled himself on top of Kevin, grabbing at his arms in an attempt to keep his brother from injuring himself. He knew he had to get help immediately!

"I am . . . Dracula," murmured a black-caped, fanged-toothed, pointed-eared monster. "I never drink . . . wine," he declared as movie-goers sat petrified in their seats.

In 1931, a novel by Irish author Bram Stoker became vividly alive on the movie screen as thousands flocked to see this re-creation of the vampire superstition which dates back to the sixteenth century.

According to the novel, a vampire looks pale, lean, and has a death-like icy touch. His eyes gleam or flash red, his ears are pointed like those of a werewolf, and his fingernails are curled and sharp. Some tales describe him as skeletal and often dressed in a black costume. His limited diet of blood gives him a foul-smelling breath. Old legends depict him with only one nostril and a barbed tongue. These creatures have the power to change their form into a cloud of mist or a bizarre nocturnal animal.

Despite modern disbelief in vampires, during the seventeenth century many thought they existed. It was believed that once a person died he could possibly return as a vampire. A corpse was often fastened in its grave with pegs or iron skewers to prevent a potential vampire from escaping.

Since the vampire was dormant during the day, graves were examined for small holes through which the monster could escape. If a grave was discovered with such holes, vampire hunters would remove the body and destroy it. This procedure took place during the daytime hours and all the hunters returned to their homes before sunset.

A young Pygmy stood in the parching equatorial African sun. He stood but five feet tall and his stature was bent from hard labor. His skin was golden brown and his hair was short and curled tightly to his head. His feet were bare and his clothes tattered. His eyes had the dull stare of a man once proud and free, but now deprived of the will to maintain his own gentle life-style.

The Pygmies are central Africa's oldest known surviving people and in the 1930s about 35,000 proudly lived in the Itiru Forest of the eastern Congo, now called Zaire. By 1957 their population had fallen to 25,000.

During the fifties, the Pygmies' ancestral forest was wastefully chopped down by lumber industrialists, robbing them of the vegetation and game they depended upon for survival. Consequently, the people were forced into the blistering sun to which they were unaccustomed. Large plantations closed in on their environment. National parks and game reserves were established, but no land was set aside to aid the Pygmy societies in their struggle for survival. Tourists brought contagious diseases to which the Pygmies had no immunity, and as a result their population continued to decline.

In 1960 the Belgian Congo received political independence, becoming the nation of Zaire. This political change brought civil war for which the nonaggressive Pygmies were the first to suffer and their number rapidly dwindled to 15,000. They became victims of new burdens such as paying income taxes, being drafted into the Zaire army, and further loss of cultural identity. By 1975 their size numbered some 3,800.

The Pygmies have a warm and gentle life-style with a dignified moral code which forbids killing, lying, theft, devil worship, sorcery, disrespect for elders, and blasphemy. They do not engage in cannibalism, mutilation, ritual murder, intertribal war, initiation ordeals, or other cruel customs sometimes associated with equatorial Africa.

FORM C

Teacher Record

STUDENT RECORD SUMMARY SHEET

Student _____ Grade _____ Sex _____ Age _____
yrs. mos.

School _____ Administered by _____ Date _____

Grade	Word Lists	Graded Passages			Estimated Levels			
	% of words correct	WR Form____	Comp. Form____	Listen. Form____	Narrative			
Primer							Grade	
1					Independent		_____	
2					Instructional		_____	
					Frustration		_____	
3					Listening		_____	
4					Expository			
5					Grade Level			
6					Science		Social Studies	
7					WR Comp.		WR Comp.	
8								
9								

Check consistent oral reading difficulties:

____ word-by-word reading

____ omissions

____ substitutions

____ corrections

____ repetitions

____ reversals

____ inattention to punctuation

____ word inserts

____ requests word help

Check consistent word recognition difficulties:

____ single consonants

____ consonant clusters

____ long vowels

____ short vowels

____ vowel digraphs

____ diphthongs

____ syllabication

____ use of context

____ basic sight

____ grade level sight

Check consistent comprehension difficulties:

____ main idea

____ factual

____ terminology

____ cause and effect

____ inferential

____ drawing conclusions

____ retelling

QUALITATIVE ANALYSIS SUMMARY SHEET

FORM_____

Level	# of Miscues	STUDENT:	Meaning Change	DATE:
		MISCUE IN CONTEXT		NATURE OF MISCUE

If additional space is needed, permission is granted by the publisher to reproduce this summary sheet.

(Student Booklet page 114)

(Primer)	(1)	(2)
1. about _____	1. ice _____	1. goose _____
2. can _____	2. before _____	2. mouse _____
3. who _____	3. another _____	3. library _____
4. with _____	4. children _____	4. teacher _____
5. some _____	5. stopped _____	5. kite _____
6. goat _____	6. hurry _____	6. cart _____
7. out _____	7. drop _____	7. different _____
8. trees _____	8. friend _____	8. anyone _____
9. father _____	9. balloon _____	9. feather _____
10. red _____	10. when _____	10. pie _____
11. green _____	11. where _____	11. sidewalk _____
12. make _____	12. those _____	12. straight _____
13. is _____	13. picnic _____	13. telephone _____
14. yes _____	14. laugh _____	14. clean _____
15. saw _____	15. farm _____	15. remember _____
16. get _____	16. airplane _____	16. wood _____
17. ball _____	17. tomorrow _____	17. summer _____
18. and _____	18. wagon _____	18. bell _____
19. down _____	19. made _____	19. gun _____
20. are _____	20. surprise _____	20. matter _____

(Student Booklet page 115)

(3)

1. clap_____
2. fright_____
3. diamond_____
4. silence_____
5. nurse_____
6. wiggle_____
7. precious_____
8. salt_____
9. bread_____
10. breath_____
11. fellow_____
12. several_____
13. unusual_____
14. overhead_____
15. driven_____
16. fool_____
17. darkness_____
18. honor_____
19. screen_____
20. they'll_____

(4)

1. canoe_____
2. hasn't_____
3. dozen_____
4. motion_____
5. pride_____
6. vicious_____
7. concern_____
8. harvest_____
9. sample_____
10. official_____
11. windshield_____
12. human_____
13. humor_____
14. decorate_____
15. slender_____
16. seventh_____
17. parachute_____
18. good-bye_____
19. dignity_____
20. trudge_____

(Student Booklet page 116)

(5)

1. prevent_____
2. kindle_____
3. grease_____
4. typical_____
5. foam_____
6. blur_____
7. mumps_____
8. telegram_____
9. vision_____
10. sandal_____
11. argument_____
12. hail_____
13. halt_____
14. region_____
15. manager_____
16. sleet_____
17. yarn_____
18. parallel_____
19. coconut_____
20. dissolve_____

(6)

1. midstream_____
2. lens_____
3. bail_____
4. college_____
5. failure_____
6. falter_____
7. width_____
8. graceful_____
9. somewhat_____
10. privacy_____
11. microphone_____
12. particle_____
13. clutter_____
14. applaud_____
15. vapor_____
16. reluctant_____
17. contract_____
18. nephew_____
19. insurance_____
20. fund_____

Primer (50 words   8 sent.)

Examiner's Introduction (Student Booklet page 117): Please read this story about a child who imagines some unusual things.

Look! It is me!

I can run as fast as a train!

I can jump over a big tall tree!

I can ride my bike as fast as a running goat!

I can see very little things far away.

I can put on a good show!

Yes, I am something!

Comprehension Questions and Possible Answers

(mi) 1. What is this story about?
   (The special kid, Super kid, etc.)

(f) 2. What does the child mean by saying, "I can run as fast as a train"?
   (can run very fast)

(f) 3. How high can this child jump?
   (over a big tall tree)

(t) 4. How fast can the child ride the bike?
   (as fast as a running goat)

(t) 5. What is meant by the word over?
   (above)

(f) 6. What kind of things can the child see far away?
   (very little things)

Miscue Count:

O____ I____ S____ A____ REP____ REV____

Scoring Guide	
Word Rec.	Comp.
IND 0–1	IND 0
INST 2–3	INST 1–2
FRUST 5+	FRUST 3+

**Examiner's Introduction
(Student Booklet page 118):**

Imagine what your Mom would say if you brought every animal you saw home to live in your house. Please read about this nonsense zoo.

> I found a lost baby turtle. I took him home so
>
> he could live in my house. A friend gave me his
>
> prize rabbit. I took the rabbit home to live in my
>
> house.
>
> I found a lost duck so I took her home too. I
>
> saw a little, cold blackbird and took him home.
>
> Then, I saw a cow who looked so sad. I took her
>
> home!
>
> But Mom said, "No! No! Not a cow!"

**Comprehension Questions
and Possible Answers**

(mi) 1. What is the child in this story doing?
(collecting stray animals)

(f) 2. What animal did the child find first?
(lost baby turtle)

(t) 3. What is meant by the phrase, "a prize rabbit"?
(the best one, one which wins honors)

(f) 4. How did the cow look?
(so sad)

(f) 5. Name the animals that the child in the story took home.
(turtle, rabbit, duck, blackbird, cow)

(inf) 6. What is said in the story which makes you think Mother didn't want a cow in the house?
(Stated: She said, "No! No! Not a cow!")

Miscue Count:

O____ I____ S____ A____ REP____ REV____

Scoring Guide	
Word Rec.	Comp.
IND 0–1	IND 0
INST 3–4	INST 1–2
FRUST 8+	FRUST 3+

Examiner's Introduction
(Student Booklet page 119):

If your pet has ever been hurt or injured, you will understand how the child in the next story feels. Please read this story.

"Look out, you'll get hit!" I yelled as Shep ran

across the busy road. "Thud!" was the noise I heard,

and then I saw my pup lying in the street. "Oh, no!" I

shouted. I felt scared inside.

"Shep is my best friend!" I wanted to cry out. I

knew that he was hurt, but he'd be all right if I could

get help fast. I knew I had to be brave.

"Mom! Dad!" I yelled as I ran straight home. I

tried to fight back the tears. But they started rolling

down my face anyway as I blasted through the door.

"Shep has been hit, and he's badly hurt!" I cried out.

"Please hurry and help him!"

Comprehension Questions
and Possible Answers

(mi) 1. In this story, what happens to the child's dog?
(gets hit on a busy road)

(f) 2. When the child first saw the hurt pet, how did the child feel?
(scared inside)

(t) 3. What is meant by the phrase, "fight back the tears"?
(to try to keep from crying)

(f) 4. Where did the child run to get help?
(ran straight home)

(ce) 5. What would happen if the child could get help fast?
(Shep would be all right.)

(inf) 6. What does the child say to make you think he loved the dog?
(Stated: Shep is my best friend.)

Miscue Count:

O____ I____ S____ A____ REP____ REV____

Scoring Guide	
Word Rec.	Comp.
IND 1	IND 0
INST 6	INST 1–2
FRUST 12+	FRUST 3+

**Examiner's Introduction
(Student Booklet page 120):**

This is a story of a new boy who has a problem and thinks of an ingenious way to solve his problem. Please read how he sets out to do this.

FOR NEIGHBORHOOD TIGERS ONLY! KNOCK ONE THOUSAND TIMES AND SAY THE SECRET WORD BEFORE ENTERING!

These were the signs which Jack read as he stood outside the neighborhood clubhouse. Jack was a new boy, and he really wanted to belong to the club. "How can I get the kids to agree to let me belong?" he thought. Suddenly he dashed home and soon returned with a bucket of yellow paint, one of black, and several brushes. He began pounding on the clubhouse door.

"I'm knocking a thousand times!" he shouted. "I don't know the secret word," he declared, "but I have something important to tell everyone! I'm the new boy," he explained. "Since the name of your club is 'Tigers,' I thought you might want to paint your clubhouse yellow with black stripes!"

All the kids thought this was a great idea and quickly invited Jack to belong!

**Comprehension Questions
and Possible Answers**

(mi) 1. Why does Jack want to belong to the club?
        (He is the new boy and wants to make friends.)

(f)   2. Where was Jack standing when he read the signs?
        (outside the clubhouse)

(t)   3. In the sentence, "how can I get the kids to agree to let me belong," what is meant by the word *belong*?
        (consent to his membership in the club)

(f)   4. What did Jack dash home to get?
        (yellow and black paint and several brushes)

(t)   5. What is meant by the phrase, "he explained"?
        (He told all about something.)

(ce) 6. Why did Jack finally knock on the clubhouse door?
        (He had something to tell everyone.)

(ce) 7. Why did the kids quickly invite Jack to belong?
        (They thought he had a great idea.)

(inf) 8. What is said in the story that makes you think Jack was lonely and eager to make friends? (Stated: He was a new boy, and he wanted to belong to the neighborhood clubhouse.)

Miscue Count:

O____ I____ S____ A____ REP____ REV____

Scoring Guide	
Word Rec.	Comp.
IND 1–2	IND 0–1
INST 7–8	INST 2
FRUST 15+	FRUST 4+

Level 4 (144 words   12 sent.)

Examiner's Introduction (Student Booklet page 121):

If you ever had a pet that you loved, then you will understand how Jody felt about Gabilan in John Steinbeck's book, *The Red Pony*. In the winter Gabilan catches pneumonia and things take a turn for the worse. Please read a retelling of one of the incidents from this memorable book.

Jody was so worried that he didn't even care to eat. He had stayed in the barn all day to take care of his sick pony, Gabilan. The pony's condition was growing worse as his breathing grew louder and harder.

At nightfall Jody brought a blanket from the house so he could sleep near Gabilan. In the middle of the night a wind whipped around the barn and blew the door open.

At dawn Jody awakened to the banging of the barn door. Gabilan was gone! In alarm he ran from the barn following the pony's tracks. Looking upward he saw buzzards, the birds of death, flying overhead. Jody stood still, then ran to the top of a small hill. In a clearing below, he saw something that filled his heart with anger and hate. A buzzard was perched on his dying pony's head.

Comprehension Questions and Possible Answers

(mi) 1. In this passage, what was wrong with Jody's colt?
(Gabilan was sick and getting worse.)

(t) 2. In this story, what is meant by the phrase, "pony's condition"?
(Gabilan's poor health)

(ce) 3. Why did Jody take a blanket from the house?
(so he could sleep near Gabilan)

(f) 4. What awakened Jody at dawn?
(the banging of the barn door)

(t) 5. What is meant by the phrase "at dawn"?
(at sunrise, at the start of the day)

(ce) 6. Why was the barn door banging?
(In the middle of the night a wind whipped around the barn and blew the door open.)

(f) 7. How did Jody try to find his pony?
(He followed the pony's tracks.)

(inf) 8. What is said in the story that makes you think Jody feared his pony might be dead?
(Stated: Looking upward he saw buzzards, the birds of death, flying overhead.)

Miscue Count:

O___ I___ S___ A___ REP___ REV___

Scoring Guide	
Word Rec.	Comp.
IND 1–2	IND 0–1
INST 7–8	INST 2
FRUST 15+	FRUST 4+

**Examiner's Introduction
(Student Booklet page 122):**

This is a story about one outstanding auto racer. The following information was derived from an article entitled, "Woman Drag Racer After Speed Record," appearing in a 1975 issue of *The Christian Science Monitor*.

"I want to be the fastest woman driver in the world," stated Shirley Muldowney. "I'd really like to go 500 miles per hour, but I'll be happy to go 400 this year and try for 500 next year," she quickly added.

Shirley, nicknamed Cha Cha, is presently the only woman licensed to drive Top Fuel cars. These cars are the fastest, the most powerful, and among the most carefully built machines in the car racing sport. Not only is she licensed to drive Top Fuel cars, but she is now one of the top challengers in the country. She has established a top speed of 241.58 miles per hour. No Top Fuel driver has reached a speed of over 250 miles per hour.

Shirley has a great deal of energy, determination, and nerve. She is confident that she can drive her car to victory. It is characteristic of her to accomplish about anything she sets out to do. A good friend has said, "It's been a long time since people thought of her just as a woman who drives race cars. She's a top driver who just happens to be a woman!"

**Comprehension Questions
and Possible Answers**

(mi) 1. What is unusual about Shirley Muldowney's career?
(She is the only woman licensed to drive Top Fuel cars.)

(f) 2. What does Shirley state to be her goal?
(She wants to be the fastest woman driver in the world by going 500 miles per hour.)

(t) 3. What is meant by the word *determination*?
(strong will to accomplish something)

(f) 4. What is special about Top Fuel cars in the racing sport?
(the fastest, most powerful, and among the most carefully built)

(ce) 5. Why is Shirley one of the top challengers in the country?
(She has established a top speed of 241.58 miles per hour.)

(t) 6. What is meant by the word *characteristic*?
(something which describes that particular person)

(ce) 7. Why don't people think of Shirley as just a woman who drives cars?
(She's a top driver.)

(con) 8. What is said in this story that makes you think Shirley will do well as a Top Fuel driver? (Stated: She has energy, determination, and nerve; she is confident she can win races; she accomplishes what she sets out to do.)

Miscue Count:

O___ I___ S___ A___ REP___ REV___

Scoring Guide	
Word Rec.	Comp.
IND 2	IND 0–1
INST 9	INST 2
FRUST 18+	FRUST 4+

Form C / Teacher Record / Graded Paragraphs

Examiner's Introduction (Student Booklet page 123): You are about to read of a very dedicated and famous black surgeon who defied medical tradition and performed unusual surgery before the 1900s. The following information was derived from a book entitled, *Black Pioneers of Science and Invention*, by Louis Haber.

James Cornish lay wounded on the saloon floor! "He's been stabbed in the chest!" shouted one horrified bystander. "Someone get him to a hospital!" another shouted.

It was a hot and humid day in Chicago in 1893. Cornish arrived at the hospital with a one-inch knife wound in his chest, dangerously near his heart. Dr. Daniel Hale Williams was called in to operate.

In those days when blood transfusions and antibiotics were unknown, chest surgery was rarely attempted since it meant a high risk of death. As Dr. Williams began to operate, he found that the stab wound had cut the heart and the sac around the heart. Dr. Williams then made history by becoming the first surgeon to successfully operate on the human heart.

Dr. Williams did not release this information for three and a half years. When he did, the newspaper headline read, "Sewed Up His Heart," and the news became known to the entire world. Not only had Cornish been discharged from the hospital a well man, but he lived fifty years after his surgery. Cornish even outlived the surgeon who had saved his life.

Comprehension Questions and Possible Answers

(mi)   1. What was Dr. Daniel Williams' unusual accomplishment?
(performed heart surgery before the days of modern medicine)

(f)   2. Where was Cornish's wound?
(in the chest, dangerously near his heart)

(t)   3. What is meant by the word *rarely*?
(not very often)

(ce)   4. When Dr. Williams found that the heart had been cut, what did he do?
(sewed it up)

(t)   5. What is meant by the phrase, "release this information"?
(give the news to the papers)

(ce)   6. What happened when Williams finally released the news?
(Newspapers printed the story, and the news became known to the entire world.)

(f)   7. How long did Cornish live after his surgery?
(fifty years)

(inf)   8. What is said in this story that makes you think chest surgery was so unusual in those days?
(Stated: Blood transfusions and antibiotics were unknown, causing high risk of death.)

Miscue Count:

O___ I___ S___ A___ REP___ REV___

Scoring Guide

Word Rec.		Comp.	
IND	2	IND	0–1
INST	10–11	INST	2
FRUST	21+	FRUST	4+

**Examiner's Introduction
(Student Booklet page 124):**

Maia Wojciechowska's book, *Tuned Out,* is a realistic exposure of the drug scene and its harmful effects. Please read a retelling of one of the incidents from this memorable book.

Jim was sixteen years old, and he thought more of his older brother, Kevin, than anyone else. He had informed all his friends that he'd not see them during the summer because he would be spending all his time with Kevin. It would be a terrific summer because Kevin was the greatest guy in the world.

But when Kevin arrived home from his first year at college something was different about him; he seemed unsettled, stayed confined to his room, and requested that Jim not disturb him. He wasn't interested in talking over old times. In fact, everything seemed to bore him.

Soon Jim discovered that Kevin had changed. Kevin smoked grass and spent his days beating the streets looking for LSD. Jim was stunned, bewildered, and to make things worse, it seemed to him that their parents didn't notice any unusual change in Kevin's personality.

Then one evening that inevitable occurrence which goes along with the drug scene happened. Kevin had taken the LSD near the time their folks left the house. It wasn't long before Jim found his brother convulsing, writhing on the floor, hallucinating, and unconsciously screaming out crazy things.

It was a frightful experience for Jim to see Kevin in such torture. He was terrorized with fear as he hurled himself on top of Kevin, grabbing at his arms in an attempt to keep his brother from injuring himself. He knew he had to get help immediately!

**Comprehension Questions
and Possible Answers**

(mi) 1. Why was Jim so concerned about his brother?
(He had discovered that Kevin was taking drugs.)

(ce) 2. Why did Jim inform his friends that he'd not see them during the summer?
(He wanted to spend all his time with his brother, Kevin.)

(f) 3. How did Jim feel when he discovered that Kevin was taking drugs?
(stunned, bewildered)

(t) 4. What is meant by the phrase, "beating the streets"?
(to search thoroughly by walking around the streets)

(t) 5. What is meant by an "inevitable occurrence"?
(something unavoidable)

(ce) 6. How did the LSD affect Kevin?
(convulsing, writhing, hallucinating, screaming)

(ce) 7. Why did Jim throw himself on top of his brother?
(to keep Kevin from injuring himself)

(con) 8. What is said in the story that makes you think Kevin's parents didn't know about his problem?
(Stated: Jim thought they hadn't noticed; they had left the house)

Miscue Count:

O____ I____ S____ A____ REP____ REV____

Scoring Guide			
Word Rec.		Comp.	
IND	2–3	IND	0–1
INST	13	INST	2
FRUST	26+	FRUST	4+

**Examiner's Introduction
(Student Booklet page 125):**

The next selection you are to read is about vampires. At one time in our history vampires and other supernatural beings were believed to exist. The following information was derived from an article entitled, "Vampires," from *Man, Myth, and Magic: An Illustrated Encyclopedia of the Supernatural.*

"I am . . . Dracula," murmured a black-caped, fanged-toothed, pointed-eared monster. "I never drink . . . wine," he declared as movie-goers sat petrified in their seats.

In 1931, a novel by Irish author Bram Stoker became vividly alive on the movie screen as thousands flocked to see this re-creation of the vampire superstition which dates back to the sixteenth century.

According to the novel, a vampire looks pale, lean, and has a death-like icy touch. His eyes gleam or flash red, his ears are pointed like those of a werewolf, and his fingernails are curled and sharp. Some tales describe him as skeletal and often dressed in a black costume. His limited diet of blood gives him a foul-smelling breath. Old legends depict him with only one nostril and a barbed tongue. These creatures have the power to change their form into a cloud of mist or a bizarre nocturnal animal.

Despite modern disbelief in vampires, during the seventeenth century many thought they existed. It was believed that once a person died he could possibly return as a vampire. A corpse was often fastened in its grave with pegs or iron skewers to prevent a potential vampire from escaping.

Since the vampire was dormant during the day, graves were examined for small holes through which the monster could escape. If a grave was discovered with such holes, vampire hunters would remove the body and destroy it. This procedure took place during the daytime hours and all the hunters returned to their homes before sunset.

**Comprehension Questions
and Possible Answers**

(mi)   1. What is the main idea of this article?
(Belief in vampires existed in the 16th and 17th centuries.)

(f)   2. What are a vampire's eyes supposed to look like?
(gleaming or flashing red)

(f)   3. How did old legends describe a vampire?
(one nostril and a barbed tongue)

(t)   4. What is meant by the phrase, "bizarre animal"?
(unique or strange)

(t)   5. What is meant by the phrase, "dormant during the day"?
(was not dangerous in the daytime)

(ce)   6. Why were iron skewers used to fasten a corpse to its grave?
(to prevent it from escaping)

(ce)   7. Why were the graves examined during the day?
(There was less danger as vampires slept during the day.)

(con)   8. What is said in this story that makes you think people in the 16th and 17th centuries
believed in and feared vampires?
(Stated: They fastened corpses in their graves with iron skewers; they searched graves
for perforations and if holes were found they destroyed the corpse.)

Miscue Count:

O____ I____ S____ A____ REP____ REV____

Scoring Guide	
Word Rec.	Comp.
IND 3	IND 0–1
INST 15	INST 2
FRUST 30 +	FRUST 4 +

**Examiner's Introduction
(Student Booklet page 126):**
Jean-Pierre Haller, a Belgian explorer and author, went to the Belgian Congo in 1957 to assist the Pygmies in their dramatic struggle for survival. The following passage was derived from an article entitled, "To Save A People."

A young Pygmy stood in the parching equatorial African sun. He stood but five feet tall and his stature was bent from hard labor. His skin was golden brown and his hair was short and curled tightly to his head. His feet were bare and his clothes tattered. His eyes had the dull stare of a man once proud and free, but now deprived of the will to maintain his own gentle life-style.

The Pygmies are central Africa's oldest known surviving people and in the 1930's about 35,000 proudly lived in the Itiru Forest of the eastern Congo, now called Zaire. By 1957 their population had fallen to 25,000.

During the fifties, the Pygmies' ancestral forest was wastefully chopped down by lumber industrialists, robbing them of the vegetation and game they depended upon for survival. Consequently, the people were forced into the blistering sun to which they were unaccustomed. Large plantations closed in on their environment. National parks and game reserves were established, but no land was set aside to aid the Pygmy societies in their struggle for survival. Tourists brought contagious diseases to which the Pygmies had no immunity, and as a result their population continued to decline.

In 1960 the Belgian Congo received political independence, becoming the nation of Zaire. This political change brought civil war for which the nonaggressive Pygmies were the first to suffer and their number rapidly dwindled to 15,000. They became victims of new burdens such as paying income taxes, being drafted into the Zaire army, and further loss of cultural identity. By 1975 their size numbered some 3,800.

The Pygmies have a warm and gentle life-style with a dignified moral code which forbids killing, lying, theft, devil worship, sorcery, disrespect for elders, and blasphemy. They do not engage in cannibalism, mutilation, ritual murder, intertribal war, initiation ordeals, or other cruel customs sometimes associated with equatorial Africa.

Comprehension Questions and Possible Answers

(mi)   1. What is the main idea of this passage?
(This Pygmy tribe is facing near extinction.)

(f)   2. Where is the Itiru Forest?
(eastern Congo, now called Zaire)

(ce)   3. What happened to the Pygmy society when their forests were chopped down?
(They were robbed of the vegetation and game they depended upon for survival.)

(t)   4. What is meant by the word *immunity*?
(condition of being able to resist a particular disease)

(f)   5. What did tourists bring to the Pygmies?
(contagious diseases)

(t)   6. What is meant by the phrase, "nonaggressive Pygmies"?
(nonhostile, nonwarlike)

(ce)   7. How were the Pygmies affected when the Belgian Congo received political independence?
(Civil war and new suffering for the Pygmies)

(con) 8. What is said in this story that makes you think no one cared enough to protect the Pygmies' rights?
(Stated: Lumber industrialists wastefully chopped down the Pygmies' forests; parks and game reserves were set aside but no land was saved for the Pygmies.)

Miscue Count:

O____ I____ S____ A____ REP____ REV____

Scoring Guide	
Word Rec.	Comp.
IND 3–4	IND 0–1
INST 18	INST 2
FRUST 36 +	FRUST 4 +

Form C / Teacher Record / Graded Paragraphs

FORM S

Student Booklet

We have five senses. They help us learn. We can learn about color if we can see. We can hear our name called out if we can hear. We can feel the joy of a soft kitten if we can touch it with our hands. We can smell good things if we can smell. We can taste the salt in the sea if we can taste. Our life would change if we did not have all five senses. It would be harder to learn.

Sounds can be made in many ways. Sound is made if someone hits a drum or shakes a paper.

We say something **vibrates** when it moves back and forth. As something vibrates back and forth it makes the air around it move. The moving air is called a **sound wave**. Sound waves move through the air. Ears can hear sound waves.

A bell begins to vibrate if someone hits the bell. The air around the bell vibrates, too. The sound waves go through the air. Small parts inside the ears begin to vibrate. The ears hear the sound. Ears can hear soft or loud sounds. Ears can hear high or low sounds, and they can hear fuzzy or clear sounds.

We say an object is **matter** if it takes up space and has **mass** or size. All things around you are called matter. Houses, school desks, flowers, and kangaroos are matter. People are matter, too.

A rock, milk, and air are matter. Each one is different even though each is matter. Each has its own size and shape. A rock is a solid. Milk is a liquid. Air is a gas. Matter can take different forms. It can be a solid, a liquid, or a gas.

Matter can change from one form to another. Ice is a solid. Ice can become a liquid called water if it is heated. Water can become a gas called steam if it is heated. Steam can become a liquid if it is cooled. Water can become a solid called ice if it is cooled.

A long time ago people became frightened when they saw a comet. They thought a comet was a sign that unpleasant events, such as an earthquake, would take place. Scientists now know that these ideas are not correct.

A **comet** is a space object made of ice particles mixed with dust. Comets probably come from the far, outer edge of our solar system. Comets can be seen only when they are close enough to the sun to reflect its light.

A comet has two parts; the head and tail. The tail is present only when the comet is heated by the sun. The tail is made of fine dust and gas. A comet's tail always points away from the sun. It can be millions of kilometers long. The head is made of ice, frozen gases, and particles of rock and metal. It could be described as a dirty snowball. The heads of most comets are only a few kilometers wide. As they near the sun, reflected sunlight makes them appear large.[1]

[1]*Accent on Science, Level 4*, Merrill Publishing Company, 1985, page 104. Reprinted with permission of the publisher.

Worms that live inside the bodies of other animals are parasites. **Parasites** are living things that feed on other living things. When some meat, such as pork, is not cooked long enough, people may get worms by eating the meat. The worms attach themselves to the intestines where they absorb food. Soon people who have parasites may lose weight and become weak. Why is it important to cook meat well?

Flatworms are the simplest worms. They have one body opening and a digestive system with intestines. Some flatworms are scavengers. **Scavengers** are animals that eat dead animals. The flatworm, planarian, is a scavenger. Other flatworms are parasites.

Roundworms are more complex than flatworms. They have two body openings, not one. The openings are connected by a long intestine. Food enters the mouth, and wastes leave from the opposite opening.

Segmented worms are the most complex type of worm. Their bodies are divided into small parts, or segments. Two body openings are connected by a long intestine. They have a heartlike organ. It pumps blood through blood vessels. They even have a small brain in the front part of their bodies. A nerve cord runs the length of their bodies.[1]

[1]*Accent on Science, Level 5*, Merrill Publishing Company, 1985, pages 27–28. Reprinted with permission of the publisher.

Your body has many natural ways to prevent disease microbes from causing infections. For instance, your skin is a barrier for microbes. They seldom pass through unbroken skin. The hairs in your nose filter some microbes out of the air you breathe. What are some other ways disease microbes are kept from entering your body?

Sometimes disease microbes do enter your body. Often when you have an infection caused by disease microbes, your body makes antibodies. An **antibody** is a chemical produced in your blood to destroy certain microbes. Your body makes a different kind of antibody for each kind of disease microbe.

Perhaps you have been sick with chicken pox. Chicken pox is caused by a microbe infection. When you got chicken pox, your body began making antibodies to destroy the microbes. As the microbes were destroyed by the antibodies, you began to get well.

Antibodies stay in your blood even after you no longer have a disease. They keep you from getting that disease again. For this reason most people have a disease like chicken pox only once.

Vaccines are used to help your body make certain antibodies. A **vaccine** is made of dead or weak microbes that cause a certain disease. When a vaccine is put into your body, you do not get the disease.[1]

---

[1]*Accent on Science, Level 6,* Merrill Publishing Company, 1985, pages 19 and 20. Reprinted with permission of the publisher.

Without motion the hands of a clock would not indicate the time of day. For every motion there is a force that causes it.

A force is needed to start something moving or to change its direction. A force is also needed to stop motion. The tendency of matter to stay at rest or in motion, unless acted on by a force is called **inertia**.

A person riding in a car has inertia. Think of a car moving at a speed of 50 kilometers per hour. How fast is the person inside going? The person is moving with the car and is not left behind; therefore, the person must also be moving at 50 kilometers per hour. If the brakes are applied suddenly, what happens to the person in the car? The person continues to move forward even though the car is stopping. If the seat belt is unfastened, the dashboard or windshield may stop this forward motion.

If you are standing in a bus, you may be thrown off balance when the bus starts to move. Your body has inertia. It tends to remain in place as the bus begins to move. If the bus goes forward too fast, you may fall backward.

All matter has inertia. Inertia is a property of matter. The amount of inertia an object has depends upon its mass. The greater the mass of an object, the greater its inertia. A sofa of large mass has more inertia than a kitchen chair. It takes more force to move a sofa than to move a kitchen chair. It takes a larger force to start and stop a bus than to start and stop a small sports car.[1]

[1]*Principles of Science, Book One*, Merrill Publishing Company, 1986, pages 107, 108. Reprinted with permission of the publisher.

Form S / Student Booklet / Science Paragraphs

Cancer is a disease in which there is abnormal cell division and rapid increase in certain body cells. Cancer can occur in any plant or animal. Dogs, cats, fruit flies, horses, as well as humans can develop various types of cancer. What causes the abnormal rapid growth of body cells? The DNA of a cell nucleus controls the growth and division of the cell. Normal cells grow to a certain size. For some unknown reason, some cells may continue to grow and divide. This rapid growth of cells leads to a formation of a clump of tissue called a tumor. A benign, non-life threatening, tumor will grow to a certain size and stop. Most moles and warts are benign tumors. A malignant tumor will not stop growing. All malignant tumors are cancers. They can cause death if they are not removed or destroyed.

Cancer cells, unlike normal cells, may separate from a tumor and be carried through the blood or lymph to other organs of the body. They can invade a new body tissue and form new tumors.

Cancer in many animals is known to be caused by viruses. Chickens are affected by a cancer of the connective tissue. Epstein-Barr viruses cause cancer of the lymph system in humans. Scientists are working to determine how viruses cause cancer.

A **carcinogen** is a cancer-causing substance. Many different chemicals are known to be carcinogens. Certain chemicals in the environment can cause cancer. Nicotine, the chemical in tobacco, can cause lung cancer. Nitrosamines, reaction products of sodium nitrate, are carcinogens. Sodium nitrate is used to preserve meat. The nitrosamines are produced during the digestive process. Too much sunlight and overexposure to X rays and other radiation can be a physical cause of cancer.[1]

---

[1]*Principles of Science, Book Two,* Merrill Publishing Company, 1986, pages 128 and 129. Reprinted with permission of the publisher.

About 2300 years ago, the Greek philosopher Democritus proposed the idea that matter is composed of atoms. Democritus reasoned that an apple could be cut into smaller and smaller pieces. Eventually he would have particles that could no longer be cut and still be apple. He called these small particles atoms, which is Greek for unable to cut.

Democritus never saw an atom. Atoms are too small for anyone to observe directly. For example, one drop of water contains millions of atoms. Scientists often propose models to help them visualize things that cannot be observed directly. The models are based on scientific theories. Much of the early work on the atomic theory was done in England. The Cavendish Laboratory at the University of Cambridge was the site of many important discoveries about atomic structure. As more information was gathered by scientists about atoms, the atomic theory was revised. Scientists are still learning about atoms and atomic structure.

According to current atomic theory, an atom consists of a small, dense nucleus surrounded by mostly empty space in which electrons move at high speeds. Most of an atom's volume is empty space. The average diameter of a nucleus is about 5×10^{-13} centimeters. The average diameter of an atom is about 2×10^{-8} centimeters. The difference in these two sizes means an atom is about 40,000 times larger than its nucleus. Consider an example of this relative difference. If the nucleus were the size of an orange, the whole atom would measure about 24 city blocks across.

Even though an atomic nucleus is relatively small, it makes up over 99.9% of an atom's mass. The nucleus of an atom contains protons. A **proton** is a relatively massive particle with a positive electric charge. The nucleus of a helium atom contains two protons. The mass of a helium nucleus is about twice the mass of two protons. The additional mass is due to neutrons found in the nuclei of helium atoms. A **neutron** is a nuclear particle that has no electric charge. A neutron has about the same mass as a proton. Most atomic nuclei contain neutrons.[1]

[1] *Merrill General Science*, Merrill Publishing Company, 1986, pages 71 and 72. Reprinted with permission of the publisher.

FORM S

Teacher Record

Science Level 1 (83 words 9 sentences)

This passage tells about our five senses, which help us learn about the world.

We have five senses. They help us learn. We can learn about color if we can see. We can hear our name called out if we can hear. We can feel the joy of a soft kitten if we can touch it with our hands. We can smell good things if we can smell. We can taste the salt in the sea if we can taste. Our life would change if we did not have all five senses. It would be harder to learn.

Comprehension Questions and Possible Answers

(mi) 1. What is the main idea of this passage?
(Our five senses help us learn.)

(t) 2. What is the meaning of the phrase, "the five senses"?
(the organs in the body that receive outside stimulus; the senses of seeing, hearing, touching, smelling, and tasting)

(f) 3. According to the passage, what can we learn about when we see?
(color)

(ce) 4. What happens when our name is called out?
(If we can hear, we hear it with our ears.)

(f) 5. What sense helps us know about the joy of a soft kitten?
(We can touch it.)

(con) 6. What is said in this passage that helps you figure out what someone's life would be like if he/she didn't have all five senses?
(If we did not have all five senses, our life would change; it would be harder to learn.)

Miscue Count:

O___ I___ S___ A___ REP___ REV___

Scoring Guide		
Word Rec.		**Comp.**
IND	0–1	IND	0
INST	4	INST	1–2
FRUST 8+		FRUST 3+

**Examiner's Introduction
(Student Booklet page 151):**

This passage tells you about sound.

Sounds can be made in many ways. Sound is made if someone hits a drum or shakes a paper.

We say something **vibrates** when it moves back and forth. As something vibrates back and forth it makes the air around it move. The moving air is called a **sound wave**. Sound waves move through the air. Ears can hear sound waves.

A bell begins to vibrate if someone hits the bell. The air around the bell vibrates, too. The sound waves go through the air. Small parts inside the ears begin to vibrate. The ears hear the sound. Ears can hear soft or loud sounds. Ears can hear high or low sounds, and they can hear fuzzy or clear sounds.

**Comprehension Questions
and Possible Answers**

(mi)   1. What is the main idea of this passage?
(how vibrations make sound, or how sound is heard)

(t)   2. What is the meaning of the word *vibrate*?
(when something moves back and forth)

(ce)   3. When an object vibrates, what happens to the air around it?
(The vibrating object causes the air around it to move.)

(t)   4. What is the meaning of the phrase "sound wave"?
(a mass of moving air caused by a vibration)

(f)   5. What vibrates inside the ear?
(small parts)

(inf)   6. What is said in this passage that helps you figure out that a person can hear when sound waves and inner ear vibrations work together?
(Sound waves go through the air, small parts inside the ear begin to vibrate, and then the ear hears the sound.)

Miscue Count:

O____ I____ S____ A____ REP____ REV____

Scoring Guide	
Word Rec.	Comp.
IND 1	IND 0
INST 6	INST 1–2
FRUST 12+	FRUST 3+

This passage tells you about something called matter. It will tell you about different kinds of matter.

We say an object is **matter** if it takes up space and has **mass** or size. All things around you are called matter. Houses, school desks, flowers, and kangaroos are matter. People are matter, too.

A rock, milk, and air are matter. Each one is different even though each is matter. Each has it own size and shape. A rock is a solid. Milk is a liquid. Air is a gas. Matter can take different forms. It can be a solid, a liquid, or a gas.

Matter can change from one form to another. Ice is a solid. Ice can become a liquid called water if it is heated. Water can become a gas called steam if it is heated. Steam can become a liquid if it is cooled. Water can become a solid called ice if it is cooled.

**Comprehension Questions
and Possible Answers**

(mi) 1. What is the main idea of this passage?
(qualities of matter)

(t) 2. What is the meaning of the phrase "an object has mass"?
(An object has size or bulk.)

(f) 3. Name some things that are matter.
(houses, school desks, flowers, kangaroos)

(f) 4. How are a rock, milk, and air different?
(One is a solid, one a liquid, one a gas; or they each have their own size [mass] and shape.)

(f) 5. What are the different forms matter can take?
(solid, liquid, or gas)

(ce) 6. What can happen to water when it is heated?
(It can change into a gas called steam.)

(ce) 7. What can happen when steam is cooled?
(It can change into a liquid called water.)

(con) 8. What is said in this passage that helps you figure out that weather might cause matter to change its form?
(Matter can change from one form to another; heat can change ice to a liquid, and a liquid to steam; cooling can change steam to a liquid and liquid back to a solid.)

Miscue Count:

O____ I____ S____ A____ REP____ REV____

Science Level 4 (172 words   15 sentences)

**Examiner's Introduction
(Student Booklet page 153):**

This passage tells us about comets and what people learned about them.

A long time ago people became frightened when they saw a comet. They thought a comet was a sign that unpleasant events, such as an earthquake, would take place. Scientists now know that these ideas are not correct.

A **comet** is a space object made of ice particles mixed with dust. Comets probably come from the far, outer edge of our solar system. Comets can be seen only when they are close enough to the sun to reflect its light.

A comet has two parts; the head and tail. The tail is present only when the comet is heated by the sun. The tail is made of fine dust and gas. A comet's tail always points away from the sun. It can be millions of kilometers long. The head is made of ice, frozen gases, and particles of rock and metal. It could be described as a dirty snowball. The heads of most comets are only a few kilometers wide. As they near the sun, reflected sunlight makes them appear large.[1]

---

[1]*Accent on Science, Level 4*, Merrill Publishing Company, 1985, page 104. Reprinted with permission of the publisher.

**Comprehension Questions
and Possible Answers**

(mi) 1. What is the main idea of the passage?
(what people know about comets)

(ce) 2. What happened a long time ago when people saw comets?
(They became frightened; they thought it was a sign of unpleasant events such as earthquakes.)

(f) 3. What is a comet?
(a space object made of ice particles mixed with dust)

(ce) 4. What happens when a comet gets close to the sun?
(The sun reflects the comet's light, and it becomes visible.)

(f) 5. What are the two parts of a comet?
(the head and the tail)

Comprehension Questions and Possible Answers (continued)

(inf) 6. What is said in this passage that helps you figure out that the comet's tail is formed from its head?
(The tail, made from fine dust and gas, is present only when heated by the sun; the reader is led to think that the warming sun melts dust and gas from the head to form the tail.)

(ce) 7. Why is a comet's head like a dirty snowball?
(because it is made of ice, frozen gases, and particles of rock and metal)

(ce) 8. Why does a comet's head appear to be larger than it actually is?
(As it nears the sun, reflected sunlight makes it appear larger.)

Miscue Count:

O___ I___ S___ A___ REP___ REV___

Scoring Guide	
Word Rec.	Comp.
IND 1–2	IND 0–1
INST 8–9	INST 2
FRUST 17 +	FRUST 4 +

**Examiner's Introduction
(Student Booklet page 154):**

This passage tells you about different kinds of worms. Read for more information.

Worms that live inside the bodies of other animals are parasites. **Parasites** are living things that feed on other living things. When some meat, such as pork, is not cooked long enough, people may get worms by eating the meat. The worms attach themselves to the intestines where they absorb food. Soon people who have parasites may lose weight and become weak. Why is it important to cook meat well?

Flatworms are the simplest worms. They have one body opening and a digestive system with intestines. Some flatworms are scavengers. **Scavengers** are animals that eat dead animals. The flatworm, planarian, is a scavenger. Other flatworms are parasites.

Roundworms are more complex than flatworms. They have two body openings, not one. The openings are connected by a long intestine. Food enters the mouth, and wastes leave from the opposite opening.

Segmented worms are the most complex type of worm. Their bodies are divided into small parts, or segments. Two body openings are connected by a long intestine. They have a heartlike organ. It pumps blood through blood vessels. They even have a small brain in the front part of their bodies. A nerve cord runs the length of their bodies.[1]

---

[1]*Accent on Science, Level 5*, Merrill Publishing Company, 1985, pages 27–28. Reprinted with permission of the publisher.

**Comprehension Questions
and Possible Answers**

(mi) 1. What is the main idea in this passage?
      (different types of worms)

(t)   2. What is the meaning of the word *parasites*?
      (living things or organisms that feed on other living things)

(inf) 3. What is said in this passage that helps you figure out there is possible danger in eating poorly cooked meat?
      (Some meat, such as pork, can contain parasites. If it is not properly cooked, the parasites can get into the consumer's body, causing severe illness.)

(ce) 4. What happens when parasites attach themselves to the intestines of a living body?
      (They absorb the individual's food, thus causing the individual to lose weight and become weak.)

(t) 5. What is the meaning of the word *scavengers*?
(animals that eat dead animals)

(f) 6. Name one scavenger mentioned in this passage.
(flatworm, or planarian)

(f) 7. What makes roundworms more complex than flatworms?
(They have two openings connected by a long intestine; food enters through the mouth and wastes leave by the opposite opening.)

(f) 8. What makes segmented worms the most complex type of worm?
(Their bodies are divided into two segments; they have a heartlike organ that pumps blood through the vessels; they have a small brain and a nerve cord.)

Miscue Count:

O____ I____ S____ A____ REP____ REV____

Scoring Guide	
Word Rec.	Comp.
IND 2	IND 0–1
INST 10	INST 2
FRUST 20+	FRUST 4+

Examiner's Introduction
(Student Booklet page 155):

This passage tells you about disease microbes and how the body deals with them.

Your body has many natural ways to prevent disease microbes from causing infections. For instance, your skin is a barrier for microbes. They seldom pass through unbroken skin. The hairs in your nose filter some microbes out of the air you breathe. What are some other ways disease microbes are kept from entering your body?

Sometimes disease microbes do enter your body. Often when you have an infection caused by disease microbes, your body makes antibodies. An **antibody** is a chemical produced in your blood to destroy certain microbes. Your body makes a different kind of antibody for each kind of disease microbe.

Perhaps you have been sick with chicken pox. Chicken pox is caused by a microbe infection. When you got chicken pox, your body began making antibodies to destroy the microbes. As the microbes were destroyed by the antibodies, you began to get well.

Antibodies stay in your blood even after you no longer have a disease. They keep you from getting that disease again. For this reason most people have a disease like chicken pox only once.

Vaccines are used to help your body make certain antibodies. A **vaccine** is made of dead or weak microbes that cause a certain disease. When a vaccine is put into your body, you do not get the disease.[1]

---

[1]*Accent on Science*, Level 6, Merrill Publishing Company, 1985, pages 19 and 20. Reprinted with permission of the publisher.

Comprehension Questions
and Possible Answers

(mi) 1. What is the main idea of this passage?
(infection from disease microbes)

(f)   2. From this passage, name two natural body barriers against disease microbes.
(the skin and hairs in the nose)

(ce) 3. What happens inside your body when you have an infection caused by disease microbes?
(Your body makes antibodies.)

(t)   4. What is the meaning of the word *antibody*?
            (a chemical produced in blood to destroy microbes)

(ce) 5. Why do people usually have chicken pox only once?
            (because the antibodies produced inside the blood when the person had the infection stay inside the body, preventing a second infection from happening)

(t)   6. What is the meaning of the word *vaccine*?
            (a preparation or matter containing dead or weak microbes injected into a living body to help build up its immunities to a particular disease, such as the small pox vaccine)

(t)   7. What is a disease microbe?
            (a disease-causing organism that can only be seen with a microscope)

(inf) 8. What is said in this passage that helps you figure out that you need to get medical care for cuts and skin abrasions?
            (The skin is a natural barrier against disease microbes; if medical care is not given, dangerous infections can enter the body.)

Miscue Count:

O____ I____ S____ A____ REP____ REV____

Scoring Guide		
Word Rec.		**Comp.**
IND	2–3	IND	0–1
INST	11	INST	2
FRUST	22+	FRUST	4+

**Examiner's Introduction
(Student Booklet page 156):**

This passage tells us about the law of motion and how it affects us daily.

Without motion the hands of a clock would not indicate the time of day. For every motion there is a force that causes it.

A force is needed to start something moving or to change its direction. A force is also needed to stop motion. The tendency of matter to stay at rest or in motion, unless acted on by a force, is called **inertia**.

A person riding in a car has inertia. Think of a car moving at a speed of 50 kilometers per hour. How fast is the person inside going? The person is moving with the car and is not left behind; therefore, the person must also be moving at 50 kilometers per hour. If the brakes are applied suddenly, what happens to the person in the car? The person continues to move forward even though the car is stopping. If the seat belt is unfastened, the dashboard or windshield may stop this forward motion.

If you are standing in a bus, you may be thrown off balance when the bus starts to move. Your body has inertia. It tends to remain in place as the bus begins to move. If the bus goes forward too fast, you may fall backward.

All matter has inertia. Inertia is a property of matter. The amount of inertia an object has depends upon its mass. The greater the mass of an object, the greater its inertia. A sofa of large mass has more inertia than a kitchen chair. It takes more force to move a sofa than to move a kitchen chair. It takes a larger force to start and stop a bus than to start and stop a small sports car.[1]

---

[1]*Principles of Science, Book One*, Merrill Publishing Company, 1986, pages 107, 108. Reprinted with permission of the publisher.

**Comprehension Questions
and Possible Answers**

(mi)   1.   What is the main idea of this passage?
(the properties of inertia)

(t)   2.   What is the meaning of the word *inertia*?
(the tendency of matter to stay at rest or in motion unless acted upon by a force)

(ce)   3. Why does a person sitting in a car going 50 kilometers per hour also travel at the same speed?
(Since the person is moving with the car and is not left behind, and the moving force is going forward, not backward, the person's inertia responds to the intensity of the moving force.)

(con)   4. What is said in this passage that helps you figure out why a person in a moving car would continue to move forward if the brakes were applied?
(A person riding in a car has inertia; for every motion there is a force that causes it; a force is needed to start something moving or to change its direction.)

(ce)   5. What is the scientific effect of a seat belt on a passenger in a moving car when the brakes are applied?
(The seat belt helps to stop the forward inertia, preventing a passenger from going forward too far, into the dash or windshield.)

(t)   6. What is the meaning of the sentence, "The amount of inertia an object has depends upon its mass"?
(The greater the size of the object, the greater its inertia.)

(f)   7. What example did the text give of an object that has greater mass than another?
(a sofa and a kitchen chair; or a bus and a sports car)

(inf)   8. What is said in this passage that helps you figure out why it takes a larger force to start or stop a bus than it does to start or stop a small sports car?
(A bus has greater mass and consequently more inertia, so the force to either start or stop it would have to be greater.)

Miscue Count:

O___ I___ S___ A___ REP___ REV___

Scoring Guide		
Word Rec.		**Comp.**
IND	3	IND	0–1
INST	14	INST	2
FRUST	28+	FRUST	4+

**Examiner's Introduction
(Student Booklet page 157):** This passage tell us about cancer and the behavior of cancer cells.

Cancer is a disease in which there is abnormal cell division and rapid increase in certain body cells. Cancer can occur in any plant or animal. Dogs, cats, fruit flies, horses, as well as humans can develop various types of cancer. What causes the abnormal rapid growth of body cells? The DNA of a cell nucleus controls the growth and division of the cell. Normal cells grow to a certain size. For some unknown reason, some cells may continue to grow and divide. This rapid growth of cells leads to a formation of a clump of tissue called a tumor. A benign, non-life threatening, tumor will grow to a certain size and stop. Most moles and warts are benign tumors. A malignant tumor will not stop growing. All malignant tumors are cancers. They can cause death if they are not removed or destroyed.

Cancer cells, unlike normal cells, may separate a tumor and be carried through the blood or lymph to other organs of the body. They can invade a new body tissue and form new tumors.

Cancer in many animals is known to be caused by viruses. Chickens are affected by a cancer of the connective tissue. Epstein-Barr viruses cause cancer of the lymph system in humans. Scientists are working to determine how viruses cause cancer.

A **carcinogen** is a cancer-causing substance. Many different chemicals are known to be carcinogens. Certain chemicals in the environment can cause cancer. Nicotine, the chemical in tobacco, can cause lung cancer. Nitrosamines, reaction products of sodium nitrate, are carcinogens. Sodium nitrate is used to preserve meat. The nitrosamines are produced during the digestive process. Too much sunlight and overexposure to X rays and other radiation can be a physical cause of cancer.[1]

---

[1]*Principles of Science, Book Two*, Merrill Publishing Company, 1986, pages 128 and 129. Reprinted with permission of the publisher.

**Comprehension Questions
and Possible Answers**

(mi) 1. What is the main idea of this passage?
          (a description and causes of the disease of cancer)

(t)   2. What is the meaning of the term *cancer*?
(a disease in which there is abnormal cell division and rapid increase in certain body cells)

(f)   3. What is the function of DNA in the cell nucleus?
(It controls the growth and division of the cell.)

(ce)   4. What causes a tumor?
(The rapid growth of cells leads to a formation of a clump of tissue.)

(f)   5. What is the difference between a benign and a malignant tumor?
(A benign tumor is non-life threatening and grows to a certain size and stops; a malignant tumor will not stop growing, is cancerous, and is life-threatening.)

(con)   6. What is said in this passage that helps you to figure out that cancer cells are extremely dangerous to a living body?
(Cancer cells may separate from a tumor and be carried through the blood or lymph to other organs of the body; they can invade a new body tissue and form new tumors.)

(ce)   7. What is the cause of cancer in the lymph system in humans?
(the Epstein-Barr viruses)

(f)   8. According to the passage, name two chemical carcinogens.
(nicotine and nitrosamines)

Miscue Count:

O____ I____ S____ A____ REP____ REV____

Scoring Guide	
Word Rec.	Comp.
IND 3	IND 0–1
INST 14–15	INST 2
FRUST 29 +	FRUST 4 +

Examiner's Introduction
Student Booklet page 158:

This passage tells us about the atom.

About 2300 years ago, the Greek philosopher Democritus proposed the idea that matter is composed of atoms. Democritus reasoned that an apple could be cut into smaller and smaller pieces. Eventually he would have particles that could no longer be cut and still be apple. He called these small particles atoms, which is Greek for unable to cut.

Democritus never saw an atom. Atoms are too small for anyone to observe directly. For example, one drop of water contains millions of atoms. Scientists often propose models to help them visualize things that cannot be observed directly. The models are based on scientific theories. Much of the early work on the atomic theory was done in England. The Cavendish Laboratory at the University of Cambridge was the site of many important discoveries about atomic structure. As more information was gathered by scientists about atoms, the atomic theory was revised. Scientists are still learning about atoms and atomic structure.

According to current atomic theory, an atom consists of a small, dense nucleus surrounded by mostly empty space in which electrons move at high speeds. Most of an atom's volume is empty space. The average diameter of a nucleus is about 5×10^{-13} centimeters. The average diameter of an atom is about 2×10^{-8} centimeters. The difference in these two sizes means an atom is about 40,000 times larger than its nucleus. Consider an example of this relative difference. If the nucleus were the size of an orange, the whole atom would measure about 24 city blocks across.

Even though an atomic nucleus is relatively small, it makes up over 99.9% of an atom's mass. The nucleus of an atom contains protons. A **proton** is a relatively massive particle with a positive electric charge. The nucleus of a helium atom contains two protons. The mass of a helium nucleus is about twice the mass of two protons. The additional mass is due to neutrons found in the nuclei of helium atoms. A **neutron** is a

Level 9 (continued)

nuclear particle that has no electric charge. A neutron has about the same mass as a

proton. Most atomic nuclei contain neutrons.[1]

---

[1]*Merrill General Science*, Merrill Publishing Company, 1986, pages 71, 72. Reprinted with permission of the publisher.

Comprehension Questions and Possible Answers

(mi) 1. What is the main idea of this passage?
(historical and current information about the atom)

(inf) 2. What is said in this passage that helps you figure out that even though Democritus could not cut the apple any smaller, he felt that particles of matter still existed?
(He had proposed the idea that matter is composed of atoms, reasoning that even though the pieces were too small to cut, matter that could not be seen constituted the makeup of the pieces.)

(ce) 3. Why do scientists propose models to help them gain scientific knowledge?
(They develop models to help visualize things that cannot be observed directly.)

(f) 4. Where was much of the early work on atomic theory done?
(the Cavendish Laboratory at the University of Cambridge in England)

(f) 5. According to current atomic theory discussed in this passage, describe the two main parts of an atom.
(a small, dense nucleus surrounded by mostly empty space in which electrons move at high speed)

(f) 6. What is the difference in size between an atom and its nucleus?
(The atom is about 40,000 times larger than its nucleus.)

(f) 7. Explain the difference in the size of an atom and its nucleus in comparative terms.
(If the nucleus were the size of an orange, the whole atom would measure about 24 city blocks across.)

(ce) 8. Since the mass of a helium nucleus is about twice the mass of its two protons, why is there additional mass?
(because neutrons are found in the nuclei)

Miscue Count:

O___I___S___A___REP___REV___

Scoring Guide	
Word Rec.	Comp.
IND 3–4	IND 0–1
INST 17–18	INST 2
FRUST 35+	FRUST 4+

FORM SS

Our country's flag is red, white, and blue. The colors come from the flag of England.

The stars and stripes on our flag have a special meaning. The 13 red and white stripes stand for our first 13 states. Each star stands for one of our 50 states. Our flag stands for the past. Our flag also stands for the present. It stands for a free nation. It stands for our country. It stands for the United States of America.

About 300 years ago, the English started 13 colonies in North America. These colonies later became our first states.

The people in those colonies had difficult lives. For transportation they often walked. Sometimes they used boats if they lived near water. Since there were no cars, it was hard for the early colonists to travel very far.

The colonial houses were much different from our houses. The houses had one large room with a fireplace. This room was used as a kitchen, a dining room, and a living room. Also it was often used as a bedroom because of the fireplace. There were no electric lights. Water had to be carried into the house.

Life for the colonists was very difficult, yet colonists thought they had a good life.

During the middle 1760's, American colonists became more and more unhappy with the king of England. They were unhappy because he took away the rights of the colonists. They were unhappy because he taxed the colonies.

In 1776, men from the 13 colonies met in Philadelphia. Some men suggested that the colonies separate from England and form a new nation. These men thought the colonies should be free.

One of the men at the meeting was Thomas Jefferson. Jefferson had read many books about government and laws. He did not speak much during the talks, but he listened carefully. He began to write the reasons for freedom from England.

Later, Jefferson wrote about the reasons why the colonists should be free. The other men liked what Jefferson had written. On July 4th, the men voted on what Jefferson had written. It was accepted and this paper written by Thomas Jefferson is called the Declaration of Independence.

During the 1600's the French settled much of eastern Canada. They called this land New France. They had heard stories about a large body of water to the west. The French thought it might be the Pacific Ocean. They wanted more land to add to the French Empire. Soon they began to look for the great body of water. This journey took them to regions that are now part of the United States. Some went south instead of west.

In 1679 a Frenchman, La Salle, began a second journey to explore the Great Lakes region. He started at the south end of Lake Michigan. He followed the Illinois River to the place where it met the Mississippi River. By 1682 he had gone all the way down the Mississippi to where it flowed into the Gulf of Mexico. He claimed the lands on both sides of the river. He also claimed the rivers that flowed into the land. He named the region Louisiana in honor of Louis XIV, the French king.

During the early and mid 1800's, there was much talk in the United States about slavery. Most of the northern states had outlawed slavery. However, in the South slaves were considered important to the plantation owners who grew cotton and tobacco. The slavery issue was not settled until Abraham Lincoln was elected president in 1860.

Until 1861, all the states had worked together as the United States. However, in 1861, leaders in the southern states believed that states had the right to leave or **secede** from the United States. The leaders in the northern and western states believed that no state had the right to secede. This difference in beliefs was one cause of the Civil War.

The states that seceded from the Union were states that used slaves. Those states formed a group called the Confederate States of America, or simply, the Confederacy. When the Civil War began in 1861, there were 11 southern states in the Confederacy.

The Civil War was very difficult because Americans were fighting Americans. In some cases brothers fought on opposing sides. After four long years of fighting, the South surrendered in April of 1865.

In the late 1700's in Europe and the United States, the Industrial Revolution was making rapid changes in the way people lived. One of history's stories of how lives changed was told in the growth of the textile industry. Textile is woven cloth.

For hundreds of years before the Industrial Revolution, farm families had spun yarn or thread and then woven the cloth. This was done in their homes. It was one way they could earn extra money. Often times, a whole family would help to make the cloth. Merchants who wanted cloth to sell in their shops supplied a family with the raw goods.

In 1773 an Englishman named John Kay invented the flying shuttle, which helped weavers work more quickly. In 1764 James Hargreaves invented the spinning wheel. His invention could produce eight threads at once instead of only one. Finally, a power loom was invented.

Soon the new machines became so big and cost so much that they needed to be located near some kind of power source. Buildings called factories were built near fast-moving streams. Instead of spinning cloth in the farm homes, workers had to leave their homes. They traveled to the factories and worked long hours away from home.

In the 1870's, some states turned their attention to public education. They passed **compulsory attendance laws**. These laws required that children attend school for a certain part of the year. By 1900, 30 states had passed such laws.

More people turned their attention to higher education during the late 1800's. One of the reasons for this was the Morrill Act, passed in 1862. Under this act, states were given public lands to set up state colleges of engineering, teacher training, and agriculture. Meanwhile, the total number of colleges grew from about 500 in 1870 to nearly 1,000 in 1900.

During these years, educational opportunities increased for both women and blacks. By 1900, nearly 100,000 women were attending college. Also, blacks had founded over 30 colleges, mostly in the South. Over 2,000 black students had graduated from these colleges.

The growing interest in education was matched by a growing amount of time spent at leisure. Greater use of labor-saving machines both at work and at home made it possible for people to have more free time. This free time was spent in a number of ways.

Americans spent a great deal of time at sports. The most popular spectator sport was baseball. In 1869, the first professional team, the Cincinnati Red Stockings, was formed. In 1876, teams from eight cities formed the National League, and in 1900, the American League was set up. The first World Series, between the Boston Red Sox and the Pittsburgh Pirates, was played in 1903.

Football was nearly as popular a spectator sport as baseball. It had first been played between teams of students from the same college. Then in 1869, the first intercollegiate (involving two or more colleges) game took place between Princeton and Rutgers.[1]

[1]*America Is*, Merrill Publishing Company, 1987, pages 457 and 458. Reprinted with permission of the publisher.

In 1955, American advisers had been sent to South Vietnam to train the army. Both Presidents Eisenhower and Kennedy sent more advisers, support troops, and military supplies between 1956 and 1962.

By the time Lyndon Johnson became President, a group of South Vietnamese Communists, called the Viet Cong, were well established in South Vietnam. They fought as **guerrillas**—bands who make war by harrassment and sabotage. The Viet Cong were getting help from North Vietnam.

In August 1964, after an attack by North Vietnamese gunboats on American warships in the Gulf of Tonkin, President Johnson asked Congress to allow him to take steps to prevent future attacks. Congress replied by passing the Tonkin Gulf Resolution. It allowed the President, as Commander in Chief, to use any measures necessary to halt an attack on American forces, stop North Vietnamese aggression, and aid any SEATO member who asked for help defending its freedom.

In February 1965, Viet Cong attacks killed several Americans. This led President Johnson to order the bombing of North Vietnam. The President also sent the first combat troops to South Vietnam. By the end of 1968, there were more than 500,000 American soldiers there. The war was costing the United States about $25 billion a year.

Public opinion was divided over the Vietnam War. Many people felt that the war was necessary to stop communism. Others felt that it was a civil war that should be settled by the Vietnamese. Still others felt that the money spent on the war could be put to better use at home. These divisions were seen in Congress, which was divided between the **"hawks"**—those who favored greater military effort—and the **"doves"**—those who wanted the war effort lessened.[1]

---

[1]*America Is*, Merrill Publishing Company, 1987, pages 656 and 657. Reprinted with permission of the publisher.

In recent years, the American economy has been changing. It has been growing steadily. The **gross national product** (GNP)—the value of all goods and services produced in one year—rose. In 1950, the GNP was $286 billion. In 1984, it was $3.6 trillion. This growth, aided by new technology, has affected the labor force and farming. Nevertheless, there are problems with the economy that need to be corrected.

One thing that has helped change the American economy is technology—application of ideas, methods, and tools to the production of goods. Technology has helped Americans make more goods with less work. It has also helped Americans raise their standard of living, and it has given them more leisure time.

One example of the new technology is **automation**—the making of products by machines that are controlled electronically. For example, machines can be used to weld parts of cars together and to print newspapers. Machines that are run by only one or two people can roll and shape steel. However, automation eliminates the need for certain jobs. This means fewer jobs and more people out of work.

Another example of the new technology is computerization. Computers were first developed in the 1950's, but they were large and expensive. During the 1960's, scientists replaced bulky tubes with small transistors, and computers became smaller and less expensive. They were used by banks, hospitals, and businesses to store and file vast amounts of information.

In the 1970's, computers became even smaller when they were powered by microchips—tiny chips of silicon smaller than a postage stamp. Soon, doctors, lawyers, housewives, students, and others were able to buy their own computers. Now, many schools and colleges require their students to own a personal computer.

Problems with foreign trade affect the economy. Over time, the United States has imported more resources, such as oil, along with a growing number of manufactured goods. Cars, radios, cameras, and hundreds of other items made in other countries are sold to Americans every year. So much has been sold that the United States has a poor **balance of trade.**[1]

---

[1]*America Is*, Merrill Publishing Company, 1987, page 732. Reprinted with permission of the publisher.

FORM SS

Teacher Record

Social Studies Level 1 (80 words   9 sentences)

**Examiner's Introduction
(Student Booklet page 178):** This passage tells us about our country's flag.

Our country's flag is red, white, and blue. The colors come from the flag of England.

The stars and stripes on our flag have a special meaning. The 13 red and white stripes stand for our first 13 states. Each star stands for one of our 50 states. Our flag stands for the past. Our flag also stands for the present. It stands for a free nation. It stands for our country. It stands for the United States of America.

**Comprehension Questions
and Possible Answers**

(mi)   1. What is the main idea of this passage?
(What do the parts of our flag mean? The flag stands for our country.)

(f)   2. Where did the colors of our flag come from?
(from the flag of England)

(f)   3. What do the stripes on our flag mean?
(the first states)

(t)   4. What does *present* mean in the sentence "Our flag also stands for the present"?
(now, at this time)

(ce)   5. Why are there 50 stars on our flag?
(because there are 50 states in our country)

(inf)   6. What is said in this passage that leads you to believe that our flag could change?
(A new state might be added.)

Miscue Count:

O____ I____ S____ A____ REP____ REV____

Scoring Guide	
Word Rec.	Comp.
IND 1	IND 0
INST 4	INST 1–2
FRUST 8+	FRUST 3+

**Examiner's Introduction
(Student Booklet page 179):**   This passage tells about life many years ago in the colonies that later became our country.

About 300 years ago, the English started 13 colonies in North America. These colonies later became our first states.

The people in those colonies had difficult lives. For transportation they often walked. Sometimes they used boats if they lived near water. Since there were no cars, it was hard for the early colonists to travel very far.

The colonial houses were much different from our houses. The houses had one large room with a fireplace. This room was used as a kitchen, a dining room, and a living room. Also it was often used as a bedroom because of the fireplace. There were no electric lights. Water had to be carried into the house.

Life for the colonists was very difficult, yet colonists thought they had a good life.

**Comprehension Questions
and Possible Answers**

(mi) 1. What is the main idea of this passage?
      (Life for the colonists was difficult).

(f)   2. Who started the 13 colonies?
      (the English colonists)

(t)   3. What does the word *transportation* mean?
      (ways of travel)

(ce) 4. Why couldn't the colonists travel very far from home?
      (There were no cars; they had to walk or go by boat.)

(f) 5. How were the early colonial houses different from ours?
(There were no electric lights. Water had to be carried into the house. Everything was done in one room.)

(inf) 6. What is said in this passage that helps you figure out that the fireplace was important in colonists' lives?
(There was one large room, which was used as the kitchen, dining room, living room, and often the bedroom.)

Miscue Count:

O____ I____ S____ A____ REP____ REV____

Scoring Guide			
Word Rec.		Comp.	
IND	1–2	IND	0
INST	6–7	INST	1–2
FRUST	13+	FRUST	3+

Social Studies Level 3 (156 words   14 sentences)

Examiner's Introduction (Student Booklet page 180): This passage tells about the time when the colonies decided to be independent from the king of England. Read about this important time in America's history.

During the middle 1760's, American colonists became more and more unhappy with the king of England. They were unhappy because he took away the rights of the colonists. They were unhappy because he taxed the colonies.

In 1776, men from the 13 colonies met in Philadelphia. Some men suggested that the colonies separate from England and form a new nation. These men thought the colonies should be free.

One of the men at the meeting was Thomas Jefferson. Jefferson had read many books about government and laws. He did not speak much during the talks, but he listened carefully. He began to write the reasons for freedom from England.

Later, Jefferson wrote about the reasons why the colonists should be free. The other men liked what Jefferson had written. On July 4th, the men voted on what Jefferson had written. It was accepted and this paper written by Thomas Jefferson is called the Declaration of Independence.

Comprehension Questions and Possible Answers

(mi) 1. What is the main idea of this passage?
      (how and why the Declaration of Independence was written)

(ce) 2. Why were the colonists unhappy with the king?
      (because he took away their rights and he taxed them)

(f)   3. In what year was the meeting?
      (1776)

(f)   4. Who was one of the men at the meeting?
      (Thomas Jefferson)

(t)   5. What does the word *separate* mean in the phrase, "separate from England"?
      (to pull apart or to move away from England; to form a new nation)

(con) 6. What is said in this passage that helps you figure out that Thomas Jefferson knew a lot about freedom?
      (He read many books about government and law; he listened carefully.)

(inf) 7. What is said in this passage that helps you figure out that the men liked what Jefferson had written?
(They voted to accept it.)

(t) 8. In this passage what does the word *independence* mean?
(freedom from England and the king; making a new nation that is on its own)

Miscue Count:

O___ I___ S___ A___ REP___ REV___

Scoring Guide	
Word Rec.	Comp.
IND 1–2	IND 0
INST 7–8	INST 2
FRUST 16+	FRUST 4+

**Examiner's Introduction
(Student Booklet page 181):**

In this passage you will read about the French a long time ago in the New World.

During the 1600's the French settled much of eastern Canada. They called this land New France. They had heard stories about a large body of water to the west. The French thought it might be the Pacific Ocean. They wanted more land to add to the French Empire. Soon they began to look for the great body of water. This journey took them to regions that are now part of the United States. Some went south instead of west.

In 1679 a Frenchman, La Salle, began a second journey to explore the Great Lakes region. He started at the south end of Lake Michigan. He followed the Illinois River to the place where it met the Mississippi River. By 1682 he had gone all the way down the Mississippi to where it flowed into the Gulf of Mexico. He claimed the lands on both sides of the river. He also claimed the rivers that flowed into the land. He named the region Louisiana in honor of Louis XIV, the French king.

**Comprehension Questions
and Possible Answers**

(mi)   1. What is the main idea of this passage?
(French explorations of the New World in the 1600's)

(f)   2. What did they call the settled land in eastern Canada?
(New France)

(ce)   3. Why did some French explorers think they should go west?
(They had heard stories about a great body of water; they thought it was the Pacific Ocean.)

(ce)   4. Why were the French so eager to explore the west?
(They wanted more land for the French Empire.)

(t)   5. What is the meaning of the word *regions*?
(section or area of land; a geographical unit)

(t)   6. What is meant by the phrase, "claimed the lands"?
(La Salle took the ownership of the land.)

(f)   7. What did La Salle claim for France?
          (the lands on both sides of the river, and the rivers that flowed into those lands)

(con)   8. What is said in this passage that helps you figure out that the Frenchmen of the time were loyal to their country and king?
          (They settled eastern Canada, calling it New France; La Salle named the new territory Louisiana in honor of Louis XIV.)

Miscue Count:

O____ I____ S____ A____REP____REV____

Scoring Guide		
Word Rec.		Comp.
IND	2	IND 0–1
INST	9	INST 2
FRUST	18+	FRUST 4+

Social Studies Level 5 (190 words 14 sentences)

Examiner's Introduction (Student Booklet page 182): Our country was once divided over the issue of slavery. This passage tells about a very difficult time in our nation's history.

During the early and mid 1800's, there was much talk in the United States about slavery. Most of the northern states had outlawed slavery. However, in the South slaves were considered important to the plantation owners who grew cotton and tobacco. The slavery issue was not settled until Abraham Lincoln was elected president in 1860.

Until 1861, all the states had worked together as the United States. However, in 1861, leaders in southern states believed that states had the right to leave, or **secede** from, the United States. The leaders in the northern and western states believed that no state had the right to secede. This difference in beliefs was one cause of the Civil War.

The states that seceded from the Union were states that used slaves. Those states formed a group called the Confederate States of America, or simply, the Confederacy. When the Civil War began in 1861, there were 11 southern states in the Confederacy.

The Civil War was very difficult because Americans were fighting Americans. In some cases brothers fought on opposing sides. After four long years of fighting, the South surrendered in April of 1865.

Comprehension Questions and Possible Answers

(mi) 1. What is the main idea of this passage?
(A nation goes to war over slavery; the nation goes to war because southern states wanted to leave, or *secede*)

(ce) 2. Why were slaves considered important in the South?
(The plantation owners who grew cotton and tobacco needed them.)

(f) 3. Who was president during the 1860's?
(Abraham Lincoln)

(t) 4. What does *secede* mean in the statement, "No state had the right to secede"?
(to leave; to not be a part of the United States)

(ce) 5. What happened when the southern states decided to leave the United States?
(The Civil War started.)

(f) 6. What were the southern states called during the Civil War?
(the Confederate States of America; the Confederacy)

(f)   7. How long did the Civil War last?
(about four years)

(con) 8. What is said in this passage that helps you to figure out that the Civil War was an especially difficult war?
(Americans were fighting Americans; brothers fought on opposing sides.)

Miscue Count:

O___ I___ S___ A___ REP___ REV___

Scoring Guide	
Word Rec.	Comp.
IND 2	IND 0–1
INST 9–10	INST 2
FRUST 19+	FRUST 4+

Social Studies Level 6 (206 words   16 sentences)

Examiner's Introduction (Student Booklet page 183):   This passage provides information about how life in the western world changed in the late 1700's.

In the late 1700's in Europe and the United States, the Industrial Revolution was making rapid changes in the way people lived. One of history's stories of how lives changed was told in the growth of the textile industry. Textile is woven cloth.

For hundreds of years before the Industrial Revolution, farm families had spun yarn or thread and then woven the cloth. This was done in their homes. It was one way they could earn extra money. Often times, a whole family would help to make the cloth. Merchants who wanted cloth to sell in their shops supplied a family with the raw goods.

In 1773 an Englishman named John Kay invented the flying shuttle, which helped weavers work more quickly. In 1764 James Hargreaves invented the spinning wheel. His invention could produce eight threads at once instead of only one. Finally, a power loom was invented.

Soon the new machines became so big and cost so much that they needed to be located near some kind of power source. Buildings called factories were built near fast-moving streams. Instead of spinning cloth in the farm homes, workers had to leave their homes. They traveled to the factories and worked long hours away from home.

Comprehension Questions and Possible Answers

(mi) 1. What is the main idea of this passage?
(how the Industrial Revolution changed lives)

(t) 2. What is the meaning of the word *textile*?
(woven cloth)

(ce) 3. Before the Industrial Revolution, why did farm families spin yarn and weave cloth in their homes?
(because they wanted to make extra money)

(t) 4. What is meant by the phrase "raw goods"?
(the wool or cotton that was spun into thread or yarn)

(ce) 5. Why did the invention of the spinning wheel speed up the production of thread?
(It could produce eight threads at once instead of one.)

(ce) 6. Why did the new machine need to be located near a power source?
(They were so big that they needed a greater source of power to run them.)

(f)   7. What was the power source used?
          (a fast-running stream)

(inf) 8. What is said in the passage that helps you figure out that the Industrial Revolution
          caused dramatic changes in family life?
          (The work had first been done in the home. When the people began working in the
          factories, they were no longer able to spend most of their time at or near the home.)

Miscue Count:

O____ I____ S____ A____ REP____ REV____

Scoring Guide	
Word Rec.	Comp.
IND ' 2	IND 0–1
INST 10–11	INST 2
FRUST 21+	FRUST 4+

Social Studies Level 7 (290 words 23 sentences)

As a result of the Industrial Revolution in the later part of the 1800's, the American economy became more prosperous.

In the 1870's, some states turned their attention to public education. They passed **compulsory attendance laws**. These laws required that children attend school for a certain part of the year. By 1900, 30 states had passed such laws.

More people turned their attention to higher education during the late 1800's. One of the reasons for this was the Morrill Act, passed in 1862. Under this act, states were given public lands to set up state colleges of engineering, teacher training, and agriculture. Meanwhile, the total number of colleges grew from about 500 in 1870 to nearly 1,000 in 1900.

During these years, educational opportunities increased for both women and blacks. By 1900, nearly 100,000 women were attending college. Also, blacks had founded over 30 colleges, mostly in the South. Over 2,000 black students had graduated from these colleges.

The growing interest in education was matched by a growing amount of time spent at leisure. Greater use of labor-saving machines both at work and at home made it possible for people to have more free time. This free time was spent in a number of ways.

Americans spent a great deal of time at sports. The most popular spectator sport was baseball. In 1869, the first professional team, the Cincinnati Red Stockings, was formed. In 1876, teams from eight cities formed the National League, and in 1900, the American League was set up. The first World Series, between the Boston Red Sox and the Pittsburgh Pirates, was played in 1903.

Football was nearly as popular a spectator sport as baseball. It had first been played between teams of students from the same college. Then in 1869, the first intercollegiate (involving two or more colleges) game took place between Princeton and Rutgers.[1]

---

[1] *America Is*, Merrill Publishing Company, 1987, pages 457 and 458. Reprinted with permission of the publisher.

(mi) 1. What is the main idea of this passage?
(social changes in American society, such as educational and leisure time)

(t) 2. What is the meaning of the phrase "compulsory attendance laws"?
(a state law that says a student must go to school until a certain age)

(ce) 3. Why did more people turn their attention toward higher education in the late 1800's?
(because the Morrill Act was passed in 1862)

(f) 4. What did the Morrill Act provide?
(States were given public lands to set up state colleges of engineering, teacher training, and agriculture.)

(ce) 5. What happened that caused more people to have free time?
(greater use of labor-saving machines at work and at home)

(f) 6. In the late 1800's, what was the most popular spectator sport?
(baseball)

(t) 7. What is the meaning of the word *intercollegiate*?
(involving two or more colleges)

(con) 8. What is said in this passage that helps you figure out that the first step toward equal rights was made in our country during the late 1800s?
(Educational opportunities for women and blacks increased; by 1900, nearly 100,000 women were attending college, and blacks had founded over 30 colleges.)

Miscue Count:

O____ I____ S____ A____ REP____ REV____

Scoring Guide	
Word Rec.	Comp.
IND 3	IND 0–1
INST 14–15	INST 2
FRUST 29+	FRUST 4+

**Examiner's Introduction
(Student Booklet page 185):** This passage discusses a time in American history during the 1950's and 1960's when the United States was involved in conflict.

In 1955, American advisers had been sent to South Vietnam to train the army. Both Presidents Eisenhower and Kennedy sent more advisers, support troops, and military supplies between 1956 and 1962.

By the time Lyndon Johnson became President, a group of South Vietnamese Communists, called the Viet Cong, were well established in South Vietnam. They fought as **guerrillas**—bands who make war by harrassment and sabotage. The Viet Cong were getting help from North Vietnam.

In August 1964, after an attack by North Vietnamese gunboats on American warships in the Gulf of Tonkin, President Johnson asked Congress to allow him to take steps to prevent future attacks. Congress replied by passing the Tonkin Gulf Resolution. It allowed the President, as Commander in Chief, to use any measures necessary to halt an attack on American forces, stop North Vietnamese aggression, and aid any SEATO member who asked for help defending its freedom.

In February 1965, Viet Cong attacks killed several Americans. This led President Johnson to order the bombing of North Vietnam. The President also sent the first combat troops to South Vietnam. By the end of 1968, there were more than 500,000 American soldiers there. The war was costing the United States about $25 billion a year.

Public opinion was divided over the Vietnam War. Many people felt that the war was necessary to stop communism. Others felt that it was a civil war that should be settled by the Vietnamese. Still others felt that the money spent on the war could be put to better use at home. These divisions were seen in Congress, which was divided between the **"hawks"**—those who favored greater military effort—and the **"doves"**—those who wanted the war effort lessened.[1]

---

[1] *America Is*, Merrill Publishing Company, 1987, pages 656 and 657. Reprinted with permission of the publisher.

**Comprehension Questions
and Possible Answers**

(mi) 1. What is the main idea of this passage?
(the Vietnamese War)

(ce) 2. In 1955, why were American advisers sent to Vietnam?
(They went to train the South Vietnamese army.)

(f) 3. Who were the Viet Cong?
(a group of South Vietnamese communists)

(t) 4. What is the meaning of the term *guerrillas*?
(independent bands or groups of fighters who make war by harrassment and sabotage)

(ce) 5. In 1964, why did President Johnson ask Congress to allow him to strengthen our military power in Vietnam?
(because North Vietnamese gunboats had attacked American warships in the Gulf of Tonkin)

(ce) 6. In 1965, what caused President Johnson to order the bombing of North Vietnam?
(Viet Cong attacks had killed several Americans.)

(t) 7. What is meant by the phrase of "others felt that it was a civil war"?
(Some Americans thought the problems in Vietnam were conflicts within the country that should be settled by the Vietnamese themselves.)

(con) 8. What is said in this passage that helps you figure out that the United States' involvement in the Vietnam War caused a lot of political strife at home?
(public opinion was divided; some felt the U.S. should fight to stop communism; some felt it was a civil war and the U.S. should stay out of civil affairs; these divisions created the **"hawks"** and the **"doves"**)

Miscue Count:

O____I____S____A____REP____REV____

Scoring Guide	
Word Rec.	Comp.
IND 3	IND 0–1
INST 14–15	INST 2
FRUST 29+	FRUST 4+

Form SS / Teacher Record / Social Studies Paragraphs

This passage discusses information about the American economy.

In recent years, the American economy has been changing. It has been growing steadily. The **gross national product** (GNP)—the value of all goods and services produced in one year—rose. In 1950, the GNP was $286 billion. In 1984, it was $3.6 trillion. This growth, aided by new technology, has affected the labor force and farming. Nevertheless, there are problems with the economy that need to be corrected.

One thing that has helped change the American economy is technology—application of ideas, methods, and tools to the production of goods. Technology has helped Americans make more goods with less work. It has also helped Americans raise their standard of living, and it has given them more leisure time.

One example of the new technology is **automation**—the making of products by machines that are controlled electronically. For example, machines can be used to weld parts of cars together and to print newspapers. Machines that are run by only one or two people can roll and shape steel. However, automation eliminates the need for certain jobs. This means fewer jobs and more people out of work.

Another example of the new technology is computerization. Computers were first developed in the 1950's, but they were large and expensive. During the 1960's, scientists replaced bulky tubes with small transistors, and computers became smaller and less expensive. They were used by banks, hospitals, and businesses to store and file vast amounts of information.

In the 1970's, computers became even smaller when they were powered by microchips—tiny chips of silicon smaller than a postage stamp. Soon, doctors, lawyers, housewives, students, and others were able to buy their own computers. Now, many schools and colleges require their students to own a personal computer.

Problems with foreign trade affect the economy. Over time, the United States has imported more resources, such as oil, along with a growing number of manufactured

Level 9 (continued)

goods. Cars, radios, cameras, and hundreds of other items made in other countries are

sold to Americans every year. So much has been sold that the United States has a poor

balance of trade.[1]

---

[1]*America Is*, Merrill Publishing Company, 1987, page 732. Reprinted with permission of the publisher.

Comprehension Questions and Possible Answers

(mi) 1. What is the main idea of this passage?
(changes that affect the American economy)

(t) 2. What is the meaning of the phrase "gross national product"?
(GNP; the value of all goods and services produced in one year)

(ce) 3. How has the coming of modern technology affected the American economy?
(Technology has helped Americans make more goods with less work; it has helped raise their standard of living and given them more leisure time.)

(t) 4. What is the meaning of the word *automation*?
(the making of products by machines that are controlled electronically)

(ce) 5. How has automation affected the American economy?
(It has eliminated the need for certain jobs, meaning that some people were put out of work.)

(f) 6. According to this passage, what happened in the 1970's that changed our society?
(Microchips were developed, and computers became available to more people.)

(t) 7. What is meant by the phrase "imported more resources"?
(Items such as oil and manufactured goods were brought into our country.)

(con) 8. What is said in this passage that helps you figure out that a poor **balance of trade** means that more goods were imported than were exported?
(Over time, the United States imported more resources, such as oil, and a growing number of manufactured goods; cars, radios, cameras, and hundreds of other items made in other countries are sold to Americans each year; so much was sold that the United States has a poor balance of trade.)

Miscue Count:

O____ I____ S____ A____ REP____ REV____

Scoring Guide	
Word Rec.	Comp.
IND 3–4	IND 0–1
INST 17–18	INST 2
FRUST 35+	FRUST 4+

Form SS / Teacher Record / Social Studies Paragraphs

CLASS RECORD SUMMARY SHEET

GRADE _____   TEACHER _____

Student	Date	Narrative Reading Level			Listening Level	Assigned Reading Text	Expository Reading Level		Comments
		Ind.	Inst.	Frust.			Science	Social Studies	

REFERENCES

Three sets of references are provided in this section. They consist of references for teachers on the correction and remediation of reading problems, references cited in the inventory, and references that provided the information necessary to write the student passages.

References on Correction and Remediation

Following these bibliographic entries on reading instruction, there is a listing of common reading problems and the pages where information may be obtained on how to solve such problems.

Barr, R., and Sadow, M. 1985. *Reading diagnosis for teachers.* New York: Longman Inc.

Baumann, J. F., and Johnson, D. D., eds. 1984. *Reading instruction and the beginning teacher: A practical guide.* Minn.: Burgess Publishing Co.

Bixby, M., Crenshaw, S., Crowley, P., Gilles, C., Henrichs, M., Pyle, D., and Waters, F. 1983. *Strategies that make sense: Invitations to literacy for secondary students.* Columbia, Mo.: Mid-Missouri TAWL.

Bond, G. L., Tinker, M. A., Wasson, B. B., and Wasson, J. B. 1984. *Reading difficulties: Their diagnosis and correction.* 5th ed. Englewood Cliffs, N.J.: Prentice-Hall, Inc.

Collins-Cheek, M., and Cheek, E. H. 1984. *Diagnostic-prescriptive reading instruction.* 2nd ed. Dubuque, Ia.: Wm. C. Brown Publishers.

Cooper, J., and Worden, T. W. 1983. *The classroom reading program in the elementary school.* New York: Macmillan Publishing Co.

Cooper, J. D. 1986. *Improving reading comprehension.* Boston: Houghton Mifflin Co.

Dallman, M., Rouch, R. L., Char, L. Y. C., and DeBoer, J. J. 1982. *The teaching of reading.* 6th ed. New York: Holt, Rinehart and Winston.

Dechant, E. V. *Improving the teaching of reading.* 3rd ed. 1982. Englewood Cliffs, N.J.: Prentice-Hall, Inc.

Devine, T. G. 1986. *Teaching reading comprehension: From theory to practice.* Boston: Allyn & Bacon, Inc.

Ekwall, E. E. 1989. *Locating and correcting reading difficulties.* 5th ed. Columbus, Oh.: Merrill.

Ekwall, E. E., and Shanker, J. L. 1983. *Diagnosis and remediation of the disabled reader.* 2nd ed. Boston: Allyn and Bacon.

Gillet, J. W., and Temple, C. 1986. *Understanding reading problems.* Boston: Little, Brown.

Gipe, J. P. 1987. *Corrective reading techniques for the classroom teacher.* Scottsdale, Ariz. Gorsuch Scarisbrick, Publishers.

Goodman, Y. M., Burke, C., and Sherman, B. 1980. *Reading strategies: Focus on comprehension.* New York: Holt, Rinehart and Winston.

Heilman, A. W., Blair, T. R., and Rupley, W. H. 1986. *Principles and practices of teaching reading.* 6th ed. Columbus, Oh.: Merrill.

Johnson, D. D., and Moe, A. J. 1983. *The Ginn word book for teachers: A basic lexicon.* Lexington, Mass.: Ginn and Company.

Johnson, D. D., and Pearson, P. D. 1984. *Teaching reading vocabulary.* 2nd ed. New York: Holt, Rinehart and Winston.

Karlin, R., 1980. *Teaching elementary reading: Principles and strategies.* 3rd ed. New York: Harcourt Brace Jovanovich.

McCormick, S. 1987. *Remedial and clinical reading instruction.* Columbus, Oh.: Merrill.

Newman, J. M. 1983. *Whole language activities.* Halifax, Nova Scotia: Department of Education, Dalhousie University.

Pearson, P. D., and Johnson, D. D. 1978. *Teaching reading comprehension.* New York: Holt, Rinehart and Winston.

Searfoss, L. W., and Readence, J. E. 1985. *Helping children learn to read.* Englewood Cliffs, N.J.: Prentice-Hall, Inc.

Smith, N. B., and Robinson, H. A. 1980. *Reading instruction for today's children.* 2nd ed. Englewood Cliffs, N.J.: Prentice-Hall.

Spache, G. D. 1981. *Diagnosing and correcting reading disabilities.* 2nd ed. Boston: Allyn and Bacon.

Wilson, R. M. 1985. *Diagnostic and remedial reading for classroom and clinic.* 5th ed. Columbus, Oh.: Merrill.

Zintz, M. V. and Maggart, Z. R. 1986. *Corrective Reading.* 5th ed. Dubuque, Ia: Wm. C. Brown Publishers.

Common Reading Problems

1. Aided Words

   Bond, Tinker, Wasson and Wasson Ch. 11
   Dechant pp. 372–373
   Spache p. 144

2. Vocabulary

   Barr and Sadow Ch. 4
   Baumann and Johnson Ch. 1, 2, 3
   Gillet and Temple Ch. 5
   Gipe Ch. 6
   Johnson and Pearson
   McCormick Ch. 7, 12, 13, 14
   Searfoss and Readence Ch. 6

3. Comprehension

    Barr and Sadow Ch. 6
    Baumann and Johnson Ch. 4 & 5
    Bixby, Crenshaw, Crowley, Gilles, Henrichs, Pyle and Waters
    Bond, Tinker, Wasson and Wasson Ch. 14, 15
    Collins-Cheek and Cheek Ch. 11
    Cooper
    Dechant Ch. 13
    Devine
    Ekwall and Shanker Ch. 6
    Goodman, Burke, and Sherman
    Heilman, Blair and Rupley Ch. 8
    Karlin Ch. 7
    McCormick, Ch. 8, 15, 16
    Newman
    Pearson and Johnson
    Smith and Robinson Ch. 8
    Wilson Ch. 10
    Zintz and Maggart Ch. 10

4. Hesitations

    Bond, Tinker, Wasson and Wasson pp. 320–325
    Dechant pp. 375–76
    Gillet and Temple pp. 184–186

5. Insertions

    Barr and Sadow Ch. 3
    Collins-Cheek and Cheek p. 83
    Dechant pp. 368–69

6. Omissions

    Collins-Cheek and Cheek p. 83
    Dechant pp. 368–69

7. Repetitions

    Barr and Sadow Ch. 3
    Dechant pp. 371–372
    Ekwall and Shanker pp. 393–400

8. Reversals

    Bond, Tinker, Wasson and Wasson pp. 284–285
    Ekwall and Shanker p. 397
    Spache pp. 144–145, 148
    Zintz pp. 84–87

9. Substitutions

    Collins-Cheek and Cheek p. 83
    Dechant p. 370
    Ekwall and Shanker pp. 393–400
    Gipe p. 82

References

Anderson, W. W. 1977. Focus on measurement and evaluation—Commercial reading inventories: A comparative review. *Reading World* (December): 99–104.

Arbuthnot, M. H., and Sutherland, Z. 1972. *Children and books.* 4th ed. Glenview, Ill.: Scott Foresman.

Beldin, H. O. 1970. Informal reading testing: Historical review and review of the research. In *Reading difficulties: Diagnosis, correction and remediation*, edited by W. Durr. Newark, Del.: International Reading Association.

Calfee, R. C., and Curley, R. 1984. Structures of prose in content areas. In *Understanding reading comprehension: Cognition, language, and the structure of prose*, edited by J. Flood. Newark, Del.: International Reading Association.

Ekwall, E. E. 1976a. Informal reading inventories: The instructional level. *The Reading Teacher* (April) 29: 662–665.

———. 1976b. *Diagnosis and remediation of the disabled reader.* Boston: Allyn & Bacon.

———. 1989. *Locating and correcting reading difficulties.* 5th ed. Columbus, Oh.: Merrill.

Freiberger, R. 1973. *The New York Times report on teenage reading tastes and habits.* New York: A New York Times Company Survey.

Goodman, K. S., ed. 1973. *Miscue analysis: Application to reading instruction.* Urbana, Ill.: ERIC Clearinghouse on Reading and Communication Skills, National Council of Teachers of English.

Goodman, Y., and Burke, C. 1972. *Reading miscue inventory.* New York: Macmillan.

Harris, A. J. 1976. Some new developments in readability. In *New horizons in reading*, edited by J. E. Merritt. Newark, Del.: International Reading Association.

Harris, A. J., and Jacobson, M. D. 1972. *Basic elementary reading vocabularies.* The First R Series. New York: Macmillan.

Harris, A. J., and Sipay, E. R. 1975. *How to increase reading ability.* 6th ed. New York: David McKay.

Irwin, J. W. 1986. *Teaching reading comprehension processes.* Englewood Cliffs, N.J.: Prentice-Hall, Inc.

Johnson, M. S., and Kress, R. A. 1965. *Informal reading inventories.* Newark, Del.: International Reading Association.

Kent, C. E. 1984. A linguist compares narrative and expository prose. *Journal of Reading* (December) 27: 232–236.

Kujoth, J. S., 1970. *Reading interests of children and young adults.* Metuchen, N.J.: The Scarecrow Press.

McGee, L. M., and Richgels, D. J. 1985. Teaching expository text structure to elementary students. *The Reading Teacher* (April) 38: 739–748.

Meyer, B. J. F., and Rice, G. E. 1984. The structure of text. In *Handbook of reading research*, edited by P. D. Pearson. New York: Longman Inc.

Piccolo, J. A. 1987. Expository text structure: Teaching and learning strategies. *The Reading Teacher* (May) 40: 838–847.

Pikulski, J. A. 1974. A critical review: Informal reading inventories. *The Reading Teacher* (November) 28: 141–151.

Powell, W. R. 1970. Reappraising the criteria for interpreting informal reading inventories. In *Reading diagnosis and evaluation*, edited by D. DeBoer. Newark, Del.: International Reading Association.

Powell, W. R. and Dunkeld, C. G. 1971. Validity of the IRI reading levels. *Elementary English* (October) 48: 637–642.

Sanders, N. M. 1966. *Classroom questions: What kinds?* New York: Harper & Row.

Spache, G. D. 1974. *Good reading for poor readers.* Champaign, Ill.: Garrard Publishing.

Tanyzer, H., and Karl, J. 1972. *Reading children's books and our pluralistic society.* Newark, Del.: International Reading Association.

Tuinman, J. J. 1971. Asking reading-dependent questions. *Journal of Reading* (February) 14: 289–292, 336.

Vacca, R. T., and Vacca, J. L. 1986. *Content area reading.* 2nd ed. Boston: Little, Brown.

Valmont, W. J., 1972. Creating questions for informal reading inventories. *The Reading Teacher* (March) 25: 509–512.

References for Passage Content

Abramowitz, L. H., and Abramowitz, J. 1981. *The United States: People and leaders.* Cleveland: Modern Curriculum Press.

Borstein, L. 1975. Woman drag racer after speed record. *The Christian Science Monitor*, Midwestern Edition (July 31).

Burnford, S. 1961. *The incredible journey.* Boston: Little, Brown.

Drewery, H. N., and O'Connor, T. H. 1987. *America is.* Columbus, Oh.: Merrill.

Gentry, J. 1973. How one town solves pollution and saves water. *The Plain Truth: A Magazine of Understanding* (January): 30–35.

Gott, L., 1973. Who's that polluting my world? *The Plain Truth: A Magazine of Understanding* (January): 25–29.

Haber, L. 1970. *Black pioneers of science and invention.* New York: Harcourt Brace Jovanovich.

Henry, M. 1972. *Justin Morgan had a horse.* New York: Rand McNally.

Hill, D. Vampires. 1972. In *Man, myth, and magic: An illustrated encyclopedia of the supernatural*, vol. 21, pp. 2922–28, edited by R. Cavendish. New York: Marshall Cavendish Corp.

Hinton, S. E. 1969. *The outsiders.* New York: The Viking Press.

Hoeh, H. L. 1975. To save a people. *The Plain Truth: A Magazine of Understanding* (January): 9–15.

Huxley, F. 1970. Zombies. In *Man, myth, and magic: An illustrated encyclopedia of the supernatural*, vol. 22, pp. 3095–96, edited by R. Cavendish. New York: Marshall Cavendish Corp.

Maple, E. 1970. East Anglican and Essex witches. In *Man, myth, and magic: An illustrated encyclopedia of the supernatural*, vol. 6, pp. 753–58, edited by R. Cavendish. New York: Marshall Cavendish Corp.

McKay, R. 1969. *Dave's song.* New York: Meredith Press.

Michaud, S., and Michaud, R. 1975. Trek to the lofty Hunza and beyond. *National Geographic* (November): 647–668.

Moyer, R. H., and Bishop, J. E. 1986. *Merrill general science.* Columbus: Merrill.

Schwartz, M., and O'Connor, J. R. 1984. *Exploring a changing world.* New York: Globe Book Company.

Smith, R. 1974. *The Lincoln library of sports champions*, vol. 12, pp. 32–35. Columbus, Oh.: Sports Resources Co.

Sportswomanlike conduct. 1974. *Newsweek* (June 3): pp. 50–55.

Steinbeck, J. 1966. *The red pony.* New York: The Viking Press.

Sund, R. B., Adams, D. K., Hackett, J. K., and Moyer, R. H. 1985. *Accent on science.* Columbus: Merrill.

Wojciechowska, M. 1968. *Tuned out.* New York: Harper & Row.

WE VALUE YOUR OPINION—PLEASE SHARE IT WITH US

Merrill Publishing and our authors are most interested in your reactions to this textbook. Did it serve you well in the course? If it did, what aspects of the text were most helpful? If not, what didn't you like about it? Your comments will help us to write and develop better textbooks. We value your opinions and thank you for your help.

Text Title _____ Edition _____

Author(s) _____

Your Name (optional) _____

Address _____

City _____ State _____ Zip _____

School _____

Course Title _____

Instructor's Name _____

Your Major _____

Your Class Rank _____ Freshman _____ Sophomore _____Junior _____ Senior

_____ Graduate Student

Were you required to take this course? _____ Required _____Elective

Length of Course? _____ Quarter _____ Semester

1. Overall, how does this text compare to other texts you've used?

_____ Superior _____Better Than Most _____ Average _____Poor

2. Please rate the text in the following areas:

	Superior	Better Than Most	Average	Poor
Author's Writing Style	_____	_____	_____	_____
Readability	_____	_____	_____	_____
Organization	_____	_____	_____	_____
Accuracy	_____	_____	_____	_____
Layout and Design	_____	_____	_____	_____
Illustrations/Photos/Tables	_____	_____	_____	_____
Examples	_____	_____	_____	_____
Problems/Exercises	_____	_____	_____	_____
Topic Selection	_____	_____	_____	_____
Currentness of Coverage	_____	_____	_____	_____
Explanation of Difficult Concepts	_____	_____	_____	_____
Match-up with Course Coverage	_____	_____	_____	_____
Applications to Real Life	_____	_____	_____	_____

3. Circle those chapters you especially liked:
   1   2   3   4   5   6   7   8   9   10   11   12   13   14   15   16   17   18   19   20
   What was your favorite chapter? _____
   Comments:

4. Circle those chapters you liked least:
   1   2   3   4   5   6   7   8   9   10   11   12   13   14   15   16   17   18   19   20
   What was your least favorite chapter? _____
   Comments:

5. List any chapters your instructor did not assign. _____

6. What topics did your instructor discuss that were not covered in the text?_____

   _____

7. Were you required to buy this book? _____ Yes _____ No

   Did you buy this book new or used? _____ New _____ Used

   If used, how much did you pay? _____

   Do you plan to keep or sell this book? _____ Keep _____ Sell

   If you plan to sell the book, how much do you expect to receive? _____

   Should the instructor continue to assign this book? _____ Yes _____ No

8. Please list any other learning materials you purchased to help you in this course (e.g., study guide, lab manual).

   _____

9. What did you like most about this text? _____

   _____

10. What did you like least about this text? _____

    _____

11. General comments:

    May we quote you in our advertising? _____ Yes _____ No

    Please mail to: Boyd Lane
                      College Division, Research Department
                      Box 508
                      1300 Alum Creek Drive
                      Columbus, Ohio 43216

    Thank you!